Making
Marriage
Simple

Making Marriage Simple

10 TRUTHS
for CHANGING the RELATIONSHIP YOU HAVE
into the ONE YOU WANT

Harville Hendrix
Helen LaKelly Hunt

Illustrated by Elizabeth Perrachione

HARMONY
BOOKS • NEW YORK

Copyright © 2013 by Helen LaKelly Hunt and Harville Hendrix
Illustrations copyright © 2013 by Elizabeth Perrachione

Published in the United States by Harmony Books,
an imprint of the Crown Publishing Group,
a division of Random House, Inc., New York.
www.crownpublishing.com

Harmony Books is a registered trademark, and the Circle colophon is a
trademark of Random House, Inc.

Library of Congress Cataloging-in-Publication Data
Hendrix, Harville.
Making marriage simple : 10 truths for changing the relationship
you have into the one you want / Harville Hendrix and
Helen LaKelly Hunt.—1st ed.
   p. cm.
1. Marriage. 2. Married people—Psychology. 3. Interpersonal relations.
4. Interpersonal conflict. 5. Man-woman relationships. I. Hunt, Helen, 1949–
II. Title.
HQ734.H492 2013
306.81—dc23   2012033304

ISBN 978-0-7704-3712-1
eISBN 978-0-7704-3713-8

PRINTED IN THE UNITED STATES OF AMERICA

Book design by Jaclyn Reyes
Illustrations by Elizabeth Perrachione
Jacket design by Nupoor Gordon

2   4   6   8   10   9   7   5   3   1

First Edition

We dedicate this book to five inspiring couples:

Ray and Nancy
Scott and Teresa
Kanya and James
Eric and Jennifer
Dan and Caroline

CONTENTS

Acknowledgments

No book is written in isolation—especially one on relationships. Many wonderful people helped us simplify as well as dramatize the concepts in this book. We'd like to begin with special thanks to Elizabeth Perrachione, who we've known for twenty-five years (and we'd never have dreamed, all those years ago, that we'd collaborate on a book like this together). She not only helped us with the spirited writing of this book, but designed what we feel are the perfect illustrations. We doubt anyone in the world could touch her talent. Thank you!

A depth of appreciation also goes to our publisher, and most specifically to our editor, Sydny Miner, for thoughtfully supporting our vision for this book. And, of course, before the manuscript was even turned in, there were many who assisted us by offering their unerring eye. Sanam Hoon and Joan Denniston's attention to detail and care for this book's future readers was evident in the input they offered. Like those holding cups of water at the side of a marathon, Bernadette Gallegos and Rachel Meltzer read many early drafts with wise feedback. Bob Kamm and Jill Fein Baker came in at just the right moments with useful input. We would also like to thank our agent, Doug Abrams, who shares our passion for healthy relationships—and understands the breadth and depth of our vision. His input as we finalized the book was extremely helpful. We feel very fortunate to have such incredible people surrounding us—supporting our vision with such passion and commitment.

We also want to offer our ongoing appreciation to the global network of Imago Therapists and all they do to help couples throughout the world. And, last (but absolutely not least!) we offer our profound gratitude to every couple out there who is honest enough to admit that their relationship could be better, and who is committed to doing what it takes to build the relationship of their dreams. We make this offering for each and every one of you.

Congratulations, You Are Part of Something Really Big!

You bought this book to make your marriage better. Rest assured it will absolutely help you do that. In this book we've distilled the key concepts of our original book *Getting the Love You Want: A Guide for Couples*, and added the most important relationship wisdom we've discovered since. Our goal is to share what we've learned in short, clear chapters. The information and processes described here can move you from conflict to connection—introducing you to Real, lasting Love.

And there is more! In the pages ahead, you will learn how to create **a new kind of marriage**. You are being invited into the forefront of what we believe is a Relationship Revolution. This short walk through the history of marriage will help explain what we mean.

MARRIAGE: AN EVER-EVOLVING INSTITUTION

Love is as old as human kind. The institution of marriage, however, is much more recent. And it is even more recently that marriage had anything to do with love. To offer a glimpse into how marriage has evolved, we're going to break up this complex history into three distinct sections:

1. In prehistory, our hunter-gatherer ancestors formed "pair-bonds" (which basically meant they "went steady") to share food and shelter. Pairing up reduced the risk of getting picked off by a saber-toothed tiger or starving when food was scarce! Successful and fertile pair-bonding literally meant survival of the wandering bands.

2. Around eleven thousand years ago, hunter-gatherers settled down, becoming farmers. The concept of "property" began to evolve. It started with land, but eventually (and unfortunately) went on to include women, children, and slaves. Marriage was an arrangement created to protect the stuff one already had, while hopefully better positioning one to acquire even more. This often meant that marriages were arranged (usually by one's parents—a scary thought for some people). Love was not part of the equation.

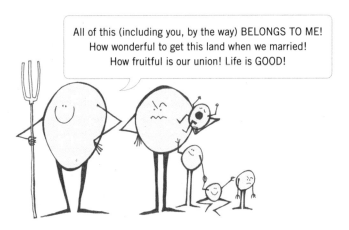

All of this (including you, by the way) BELONGS TO ME! How wonderful to get this land when we married! How fruitful is our union! Life is GOOD!

3. In the eighteenth century the romantic marriage was born. Instead of being imposed by the moral constraints of a patriarchal society, marriage was now a personal

choice. Individuals entered their relationships with newly recognized needs. But marriage didn't come with a how-to manual. And the self-help movement was a long way off. This left couples in the dark about how to identify their needs or ask for what they wanted. Enter: conflict. The divorce rate in the United States rose to 50 percent in the 1970s, where it has hovered for the last forty years.

The romantic marriage may not have come with a manual, but it did come with a relic of the arranged marriage: gender inequality. This perpetuated the uneven balance of power that was typical of the old kind of marriage. We call it the dominator/submissive model. The more opportunities opened up for women, the more this model was threatened. Submission became a tough sell.

Both partners wanted to be dominant. Each assumed: "You and I are one, and *I'm* the one!"

What comes next in the evolution of marriage is what we've been helping couples build for decades: a **Partnership Marriage.** In a Partnership Marriage, both partners are free and equal. They consciously promote each other's psychological and spiritual growth. In so doing, they experience the ultimate communion possible between humans.

As marriage and family educators with decades of experience, we can assure you that creating this model can be challenging. Though we've been married to each other for over thirty years, it certainly was for us.

Just over ten years ago we had a bold—and scary—awakening. Though we were marriage experts, we woke one day to a marriage in shambles. We had created Imago Therapy. We had helped thousands of other couples around the world heal their marriages. But we were not practicing what we preached. Who we appeared to be in public was very different from how we were at home. We were arguing a lot. Boy, did we feel like hypocrites!

So, we decided to put ourselves through the exercises and techniques we'd created for others. And the same magic we'd seen so many other couples experience became ours. We were able to re-create our previous intimacy, but on an even deeper, more profound level. Our marriage finally became the relationship of our dreams.

We believe everyone has the capacity to create this kind of relationship. And this book will help you achieve it. **You are on the threshold of the next evolution in marriage—one that has profound possibilities for you as a person and for the health of**

our world. It is only now, at this moment in time, that a Partnership Marriage is even possible. We truly believe if you practice the concepts outlined in this book, you will create the marriage of your dreams. And you will be joining thousands of other couples who are quietly working on this Relationship Revolution.

Helen LaKelly Hunt and Harville Hendrix

How to Use This Book

HARVILLE AND HELEN

Each chapter in this book offers an essential truth about marriage that we've learned from our decades of working with couples. Each chapter also ends with a simple exercise designed to help you put the concepts you're learning into practice. And at the end of the book, we've put all the exercises together into a comprehensive exercise program.

Transforming your marriage will take effort on your part. Sometimes the results will feel instantaneous. Sometimes it will feel as if you're not making any progress at all. *The important thing is to stick with it.* When our marriage was in trouble, we spent time each day putting ourselves through the exercises you'll find in this book. To be successful, you'll need to create your own kind of daily practice as well.

If instead of feeling excited, you're rolling your eyes, we completely understand. A lot of time and energy is spent finding the perfect mate. And many (if not most!) of us assume that once we've said "I do," the work is over. The idea of having to spend time focused on our most important relationship may seem strange, and maybe even depressing. This is especially true when our relationship feels at all uncomfortable.

When we first started focusing on our own healing process, our relationship was a mess. We both knew a lot about marriage—*in theory*. But we didn't know how to live what we knew. And when we disagreed on something, neither of us would budge an inch. To make our points, we'd analyze and blame each other. If you had looked up "stubborn mule" in the dictionary, you'd have found our pictures! We were so angry with each other. The last thing we wanted to do was spend time together each night, working on exercises.

The stalemate of a relationship that
is badly in need of healing.

Boy, were we pleasantly surprised! Getting started wasn't nearly as hard as we thought it would be. Each night our relationship felt a little bit better than the night before. Then, suddenly, we experienced a *huge* shift. For the first time in a long time, we found that we actually loved being together.

Building a new way of relating to each other is a lot like developing muscles. It takes intention and daily work. Maybe you'll start by reading through the book once. Some of you may just dive right in with Truth #1, Romantic Love Is a Trick, followed by the exercise. You can follow the exercises after each chapter, or use the complete program at the back of the book, which includes space for you to record your thoughts and insights (see page 150). Of course, each of you is also welcome to get a notebook or binder to record the work you do. You can even purchase two copies of the book (after all, we don't want you fighting over which one of you gets to read it at a particular time!).

We also encourage you to read through the book several times and repeat the exercises. You can do this by starting again at the beginning or choosing a chapter and exercise that feels right to you in that moment. Why are we so focused on your continuing the exercises? Because each time you work through them you will learn something new. This is the work of growing Real Love in your life, and co-creating the marriage of your dreams.

Don't worry, though, this process doesn't have to be a grueling marathon. As little as ten to twenty minutes a night together, reading a chapter and doing one of the exercises, will multiply into huge gains. You don't even have to finish a chapter in a night. You can work on one for several days. Choose the pace that's right for you.

You created your marriage together, and we feel the ideas and exercises in this book work best when partners commit to doing the work together. But don't be discouraged if your partner doesn't want to participate. One person CAN shift the dynamics in a relationship. So if you're interested in this book and your partner isn't, we say, "Go for it!"

Romantic Love Is a Trick

HELEN

Although Harville and I come from very different worlds, when we fell in love, we had *so much* in common. Both of us were divorced. In addition, we each had two children, were passionate about psychology, and loved BBQ. We even had the exact same idea of our ideal vacation: driving around the United States in a rented RV with our newly blended family. Imagine how compatible we (thought we) were!

I can't remember a single thing we disagreed on.

Ahhh, the splendor of a newly budding relationship!

One minute you're involved in your life as you know it, when suddenly you see *the one*. Your eyes meet (perhaps across a crowded room). Heart palpitations start. And the fairy tale of romance begins. Flowers, batting eyelashes, shared meals, laughter. Sunset walks and little love gifts to each other. You spend hours looking forward to your next time together. Maybe you'll see a movie or simply hang out—talking about everything and nothing.

Each of you finds yourself saying: "It feels like I've known you forever. . . ." And in some ways you have. This new person has some very strong similarities to your childhood caregivers.

Now this "falling in love" business might not be so intense for everyone. For some, it's more gradual. But either way, you begin to think about each other a lot. Being apart feels unbearable. So you text and call each other frequently. When together, you seem to know each other's thoughts. You complete each other's sentences. You know exactly what the other one wants because, well, it's exactly what you want too!

The early stage of a romance brings out the best in people. Both homes are always tidy. Personal grooming is done with special care. Neither one of you burps around the other person. Before you even know what's happening, you've fallen head over heels in LOVE.

Romantic Love that is . . .

It is a mysterious attraction: you feel moments of absolute ecstasy!

Unfortunately this bliss doesn't last.

FROM ECSTASY TO AGONY

Romantic Love sticks around long enough to bind two people together. Then it rides off into the sunset. And seemingly overnight, your dream marriage can turn into your biggest nightmare.

Romantic Love rides off into the sunset.

Now, once in the throes of full-blown Romantic Love, you can do no wrong. When Romantic Love fades however, it feels like you can do no right. The person who was once your greatest fan can become your worst critic. Adoration is replaced by nagging. You notice yourself thinking, "Who IS this person I married? We used to be so compatible. We agreed on everything." The pit of your stomach churns. And you ask yourself, "How can my partner think that way, act that way, say those things? They *fooled* me into believing they were someone else!"

When rudely awakened from the dazzling dream of compatibility, people can get *very* grumpy. Desperate to end the pain and disappointment Romantic Love leaves behind, many couples get divorced. Others who decide not to do the mind-numbing work of dividing up the stuff may stay together. But they wind up living parallel lives, without any true connection. They assume this is as good as it gets. But secretly they think something must be terribly wrong.

Is this who I married?! Something is terribly wrong.

Let us reassure you, *nothing has gone wrong.*

Romantic Love is just the first stage of couplehood. It's *supposed* to fade.

Romantic Love is the powerful force that draws you to someone who has the positive and negative qualities of your parents or caregiver (this includes anyone responsible for your care as a child, for example: a parent, older sibling, grandparent, or babysitters.). You felt like you knew your partner forever when you first met because they have the positive qualities of your parents. And because they also have your parents' negative qualities, you wind up feeling irritated and disappointed by your partner. This is why agony can replace the initial ecstasy. Why relationships can get so painful and hard.

Whoa! The idea that your partner is really a composite of your parents can be a bit upsetting at first. Though we love our parents, most of us got over (consciously) wanting to marry them when we turned five or six. Then, when we hit our teenage years, all we wanted was our freedom. But the fact is, we're unconsciously drawn to that special someone with the best and worst character traits of all of our caregivers combined. We call this our "Imago"—the template of positive and negative qualities of your primary caregivers.

What goes on behind the scenes.

If you're reading this and thinking, "But wait, there is no resemblance between my partner and my parents," let us clarify: Your partner may not *look* like your parents, and on the surface they may not *act* like your parents. But you will end up *feeling the same feelings you had as a child* when you were with your parents. This includes the sense of belonging and the love you felt. But it also includes the experience and upset of not getting all your needs met.

RELIVING CHILDHOOD

We call the result of not getting all of your needs met your "childhood wounding." You become sensitive in the present to what was missing in the past. Our unconscious mind is set up so that **the only way to heal these wounds is to have someone with traits like our caregivers learn how to give us what we needed—and missed out on—in childhood**. Though frustrating to endure, this design of relationship has a wondrous plan: to heal each other's childhood wounds.

Rest assured that when we talk about childhood wounding, we're not blaming anyone's parents (ours or yours). The reality is that nobody's parents were perfect. Ask any one of our six kids if we were perfect, and they will assure you we're *certainly* not! But even when parents are great, there are ways their parenting misses the mark. In other words, it's impossible to parent "perfectly."

So whether your parents were lousy, or if their wounding was more subtle, the results generally fall into two categories. Your parents were either overinvolved, which left you feeling controlled and smothered.

Or your parents were underinvolved, which left you feeling abandoned.

As a young girl, I felt smothered by the expectations of others. My parents required me to be sweet and thoughtful to everyone, no matter how I really felt. Born and raised in the South, my whole culture expected me to be a gracious Southern Belle who pleased others. I was even taught how to execute a perfect curtsey—seriously, I was expected to *bow* to others. Busy volunteering at the hospital, my mother was rarely around when I got home from school. And, like her, I was expected to volunteer the majority of my free time.

Now fast-forward to my marriage.

You'd think I'd be the perfect wife, caring for Harville in every way. . . .

Well, the truth is yes . . . and no.

When we got married, I vowed to be the best wife I could be to Harville. Utterly devoted, I prided myself on paying attention to all the details of his life—every single one of them. Pretty soon, I felt like I knew him better than he knew himself. (Oh dear, watch out!)

When friends asked Harville a question, I'd often proudly jump in and answer. I'd set out his breakfast and pridefully cook dinner for him without asking what he wanted. I didn't have to ask. Because I already knew. Given his love of *Star Trek*, I just knew he'd be delighted with the *Star Trek* mugs and bath towels I surprised him with from time to time. I was so attentive to Harville that if you wanted to know how he was doing, all you had to do was ask me.

Given all I was doing for him, I assumed he felt so lucky to be married to me. Then one day, Harville did something SO completely out of character. He SNAPPED! I'd never seen him so angry. I was shocked. Hurt. And *so* confused. How could he not appreciate *all* that I was doing? After he calmed down, he explained that in all my efforts, I'd never actually *asked* him what he wanted. This was stunning feedback. I'd assumed I already knew, but instead Harville felt utterly eradicated.

In spite of my many efforts, I was failing to meet any of Harville's real needs. I was doing things for him, but I wasn't connecting with him.

The patterns from my childhood wounding fit perfectly with Harville's. Both of Harville's parents died when he was young and he was sent to live with his older sister, Rosa Lee, when he was six. She tried to do everything she could for him. And she was great in many ways. But she had other children to care for. And she was his older sister. So she wasn't as attuned to Harville as his mother had been. How could she be? As a result, Harville felt very lonely. His primary childhood wounding was abandonment.

My doing things for Harville without really being connected with him brought up these same childhood feelings. Once again he was being abandoned, but this time by his wife.

It wasn't a mistake that our childhood wounding fit together so well. **Remember, when Romantic Love strikes, you will be** drawn to a person whose behaviors make you re-experience the feelings you had with your caregivers.

So remember, your unconscious mind chose your partner. It knew that in order to heal your childhood wounds, you had to feel these emotions again as an adult. Marriage gives you this chance to relive memories and feelings from your childhood, *but with a different, happier outcome.* As a child you were helpless. As an adult, you have power. You can work with your partner so that each of you gets your needs met.

BUT HERE'S SOME GOOD NEWS

All this may seem like a terrible tangle. But since partnership is designed to resurface feelings from childhood, it means that **most of the upset that gets triggered in us during our relationship is from our past.** Yes! About 90 percent of the frustrations your partner has with you are really about *their* issues from childhood. That means only 10 percent or so is about each of you right now. Doesn't that make you feel better?

MYSTERY DECODED!

Romantic Love delivers us into the passionate arms of someone who will ultimately trigger the same frustrations we had with our parents, but for the best possible reason! Doing so brings our childhood wounds to the surface so they can be healed.

You'd think that with this potential for healing, your relationship would get a whole lot better in a hurry. And eventually it will get a whole lot better.

But there's some challenging work to be done first.

Truth #1: Romantic Love Is a Trick

EXERCISE: THEN AND NOW

First:

1. Write down the frustrations you remember that you had with your childhood caregivers and how you felt (you can use "Frustrations Then and Now" on page 157, which is part of the exercise program at the back of the book). The frustrations can be a specific event or a general experience.

    Reminder: Caregivers include whoever was responsible for your care when you were a child, for example, a parent, older sibling, relative, or babysitter.

2. List the ongoing frustrations you have with your partner and how these make you feel. List as many as you can— including both petty annoyances and those things that really irritate you.

3. Look over the two lists, noting any similarities.

Then:

Talk over the similarities between the two lists with your partner. As you share, you'll notice the curiosity growing between you. It's hard to feel curious and frustrated at the same time. In the exercise for Truth #7 (Negativity Is a Wish in Disguise) you will practice how to turn the more challenging frustrations you have with your partner into specific requests for growth and healing.

And Remember:

*Ninety percent of our frustrations with our partner
come from experiences from our past.
That means only 10 percent of the frustrations
you currently have are about each other.*

Incompatibility Is Grounds for Marriage

HARVILLE

Why will the work on your marriage be challenging? Not only is the person you're married to like your parents, but the two of you are also incompatible. It's as if there is a universal design and, mysteriously, our incompatibility seems to be a key piece of this plan. As you'll see, incompatibility plays a crucial role in preparing you and your partner to meet each other's needs.

This is why we say that **incompatibility *is* grounds for marriage.**

And, honestly, compatibility is grounds for boredom.

We've seen it time and again. People want to believe they've fallen in love with someone who is a lot like them. But the fact is we're drawn to people who are, in certain ways, our polar opposite. This is why Romantic Love needs to be such a powerful force. Without it, we'd see the truth of our incompatibility right away—and run screaming in the other direction!

Helen and I were *really* incompatible. I grew up on a sharecropper's farm in rural Georgia. She grew up in a mansion overlooking a lake in Dallas. I was dirt poor. She was Texas-oil rich. My father died just after I was born, leaving my mother alone with nine children on a mortgaged one-hundred-acre farm. Mom died when I was six years old. One of the few things Helen and I had in common was this: I grew up an orphan in the care of my older sisters; she grew up "orphaned" in a house with busy household staff and even busier parents.

Helen is a nester. I am a wanderer. She is internal, and I'm oriented to the outer world. On a car trip, I'd say, "Isn't this scenery great?" Only then would she look up from her needlepoint. Helen has a minimal relationship to time, and I am obsessively punctual. If she knocks and a door doesn't open, she keeps knocking. I go to another door. She likes her vegetables soft. I like mine barely cooked or raw.

Helen is intuitive and understands complexity immediately. I'm logical. By the time I get to the solution, she's at the finish line waiting for me to arrive. Helen is a great multi-tasker. That used to drive me nuts! I'm still better when I focus on one thing at a time.

There's an old song from the movie *My Fair Lady*, "Why Can't a Woman Be More Like a Man?" I can't tell you how many times I've lamented, "Why Can't Helen Be More Like Me?" Unfortunately, this kind of lament can only lead to one thing. . . .

ENTER THE POWER STRUGGLE

"You never . . ."
"You ALWAYS . . ."
"You're such a . . ."

Welcome to the dark valley of the Power Struggle. Each of you is deeply entrenched in believing you're right. If only your partner would see how truly wonderful you are. Oh, and also agree to do everything you've asked for (or hinted at, or privately wished for but haven't said), exactly the way you want them to do it. Then everything would be FINE. The Power Struggle is absolutely miserable. But, guess what? Yes, you're catching on. . . .

This, too, is supposed to happen!

The Power Struggle always shows up after Romantic Love fades. And like Romantic Love, the Power Struggle has a purpose. Your incompatibility is ultimately what will make your marriage exciting (once you get over your need for sameness, that is). **The tension of opposites produced by this incompatibility is vital to the work of healing your childhood wounds.** It gives you the energy to work through your problems. **And helps each of you build psychological and emotional strength.**

INCOMPATIBILITY DECODED

"But wait a minute," you may be thinking, "my partner and I actually *are* compatible in a lot of ways. We love the same kind of food, the same type of vacations, and our upbringings were very similar. . . ."

Yes, you and your partner may have a lot of things in common. But we've found that couples are incompatible in two basic ways, how they: (1) relate to structure versus freedom, and (2) handle stress and conflict.

When it comes to structure versus freedom, Helen and I have very different feelings. On the weekends we have off together, the first thing Helen wants to do is plan everything out. She'll read movie and restaurant reviews. Then she'll come to me with questions about which tickets to buy and what reservations to make. What I've come to understand is that the structure helps Helen enjoy our free time together more. She can relax and really enjoy herself once the plans are in place.

I, on the other hand, prefer our weekends off to be unstructured. It's not that I want to stay home and stare at a wall the whole time. It would even be fine with me if Helen and I wound up at one of those movies or restaurants she spent time researching. I just value spontaneity. It's not fun for me to be locked into a specific activity at a specific time in advance. I want to relax and meander with no fixed destination in mind. This used to be a real issue between us, until we found ways to enjoy our weekends together that satisfied both our needs.

THE TURTLE AND THE HAILSTORM

So how do two incompatible people learn to live together? First, it's important to recognize your differences in a nonjudgmental way. Understand that you're going to have opposite attitudes about many things. And neither one of you is wrong. Once you really get this, you can creatively design joyful life patterns *together*.

Which brings us to point #2. There is a way to successfully navigate your relationship when either or both of you are feeling stressed out.

Early in our work, Helen and I discovered that people's reaction to stress and conflict fall into one of two categories: **Minimizing** or **Maximizing**. When Minimizers are anxious, they tend to pull their reactions deep inside. They contain their energy. We call this person the **Turtle**, because their pulling inward is similar to a turtle retreating into its shell. When Maximizers are anxious, they tend to express themselves loudly to whoever is in hearing range. We call this person the **Hailstorm**—because when you're on the receiving end, it can feel as though you're getting pelted with golf-ball-sized hail.

Turtles need distance. They want freedom. They like to spend time alone, lost in their own thoughts. This is how they recharge. They process their feelings quietly on the inside, reflecting carefully before offering input. They are the ones who usually keep things on an even keel. They're great at reminding people to relax if tensions get high. From the outside looking in, Turtles seem to putter along not getting much accomplished. But the "slow and steady wins the race" adage absolutely holds true for them. All they need is for you to trust them and let them loose with some uninterrupted time, and Turtles can move mountains.

Hailstorms, on the other hand, thrive on contact. Their energy flows outward, and they prefer to process their feelings with others. They are wonderful at caring for family dynamics. In fact, it was probably a Hailstorm who bought this book! Rather than carefully analyzing things, Hailstorms respond in the moment. And they intuitively have great ideas and flashes of insight. Having fun with their mate—going to a movie, throwing a party—is a great way for Hailstorms to recharge. Plus, you don't have to worry about whether they'll get things done. They have to do lists. And they *really* enjoy being able to cross things off their lists.

> So I was talking with a friend yesterday while making this new dish for dinner . . . I realized that this dish would be perfect for a fund-raiser and thought maybe we could do that for the camp our kids attended this past summer . . . and I ran into someone at the park yesterday who puts together events and their kids went to the same camp and they love the idea of helping with the event . . .

The Hailstorm: constantly thinking about and doing fifteen things at once.

When left on autopilot, the Turtle and Hailstorm will drive each other CRAZY. But the wonder of it all is that **Turtles and Hailstorms almost always marry each other.** Sometimes it's very clear which is the Turtle and which is the Hailstorm. **For others, it may not be so obvious until issues arise.** Like powerful magnets, these opposite energies are passionately and hopelessly drawn to each other. This is true for every couple we've ever met—and true for Helen (the Hailstorm) and me (the Turtle) as well.

When I am facing a stressful situation, I need time alone to process the issue. This is how insights come to me. When facing the same issue, Helen processes outwardly by talking through her feelings. She looks at the situation from one vantage point, then another, and another, and processes them all with me before settling on one.

Much of the time, we found ways to accommodate both styles. But when I became overloaded, I needed to withdraw. This drove Helen nuts! She felt that I disappeared. So her Hailstorm would wake up and start hailing to get my attention. This did not help me one bit!

Helen began to see that the harder she hailed, the more I withdrew. The idea of backing off was challenging for her. One day Helen had a flash of insight. She loves to needlepoint, and decided that whenever she felt me withdraw, she'd start a needlepoint project. This would give her something to focus on (instead of me), which would make it easier for her to back off and give me the time I needed.

Now that she's learned to channel her energy this way, she gets a fully restored and resourceful partner for problem solving. And she gets a grateful one too. I really appreciate that she's learned to respect that I need space before I can re-engage with my best self. (And our kids and grandkids have also benefited—because each of them now has a gorgeous needlepoint Christmas stocking!)

Like the trick of Romantic Love, Turtle/Hailstorm physics are a law of nature. It always works exactly like this: The deeper a Turtle withdraws into its shell, the more a Hailstorm will hail. The more the Hailstorm hails, the deeper the Turtle withdraws.

SO REMEMBER! YOU'VE GOT THE POWER TO CHANGE

A major turning point came when Helen and I finally realized that we didn't have to be victims of the Turtle/Hailstorm dynamic. We had control over how much her Hailstorm hails, and how much my Turtle withdraws. *Yes, you and your partner have the power to make this law of nature work on your behalf.*

Here's what we've learned. . . .

All you Hailstorms out there: Of course you want to storm and stomp when your Turtle retreats inside their shell. But don't! It won't get you what you want. Turtles withdraw because they feel flooded.

Other behaviors that upset the Turtle are blaming them for something that's gone wrong in the relationship or persuading them to do what you want. Turtles hate being analyzed. Hailstorms can also energetically take up most of the space in a relationship. This leaves the Turtle feeling shut out. Stick with any of these behaviors, Hailstorm, and your Turtle will stay hunkered down in their shell.

WHY are you hiding in your shell?! What did I DO? I wasn't ATTACKING you . . . I only SUGGESTED that you might be a bit too sensitive about this ONE teeny issue. Can't you see that the idea I had about the thing we were discussing the other night made the MOST SENSE?!?!?!?!?! Hey, are you hyperventilating?

Want your Turtle to emerge? Make it safe for them. Appreciate out loud all that they do. They are proud that they offer stability and keep order in their home. Recognize these gifts. Once they feel safe, there's no reason for them to hide. Give them a little shell time and they'll soon come out and connect (after all, it gets lonely in their shell after a while!).

One more point about Turtles. Pushed to their limits, they become Snapping Turtles! It may take a while to get them to this point. But once they reach it, watch out! It's not a pretty sight.

And now for you Turtles out there: When you see the dark clouds of the Hailstorm gathering, of course you want to hide. Don't! To stop the hail from denting your shell, be courageous and stick your neck out. Hailstorms hail because they're overwhelmed. They often feel like they're holding the weight of the world. And when you retreat, the Hailstorm feels even more alone. So the minute you hear a rumble, give them your full attention. Offer kindness and support. Give them a flower, write them a note of appreciation, or acknowledge their feelings.

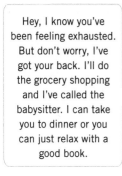

Hey, I know you've been feeling exhausted. But don't worry, I've got your back. I'll do the grocery shopping and I've called the babysitter. I can take you to dinner or you can just relax with a good book.

Wow, THANK YOU! I can't tell you how much this means to me . . .

The most important thing for Turtles to remember is to communicate gently with their Hailstorm. This is true all the time, and especially when either one of you feels overwhelmed or unappreciated. Assure the Hailstorm that you've got their back. Once they realize they can rely on you, the dark clouds will disperse and the sun will shine once again.

"CALM" HAILSTORM, MEET THE "SNAPPY" TURTLE!

So if driving each other crazy is the worst-case scenario, what's the best-case scenario? It's when the Turtle and Hailstorm learn how to dance together. And they do this by teaching each other what they know best. Turtles need to learn how to push their energy out and "show up." This means expressing themselves out loud and clearly, like the Hailstorm does. And Hailstorms need to learn the Turtle's wisdom of stepping back and containing their energy. This exchange helps each one gain important skills—and (dare we say) become more like the other.

Although our incompatibility is largely what draws us to our partner (unconsciously, of course), ironically, both partners need to learn how to be more like each other. And this includes those parts they find most annoying!

As the Turtle becomes more storm-like, and the Hailstorm becomes more turtle-like, balance is restored. In addition, these newly cultivated skills help each of you become better human beings in the world.

It's amazing to realize that we hold the key to how much our Turtle withdraws and how hard our Hailstorm hails. Working with this incompatibility helps us heal each other's childhood wounds. **Giving our partner what they need grows new qualities within ourselves, which helps us build psychological and emotional strength.** That we can do this for each other—acting as both catalysts and companions on this journey—is the true mystery and miracle of love relationships.

Truth #2: Incompatibility Is Grounds for Marriage

EXERCISE: TAMING THE HAILSTORM AND COAXING OUT THE TURTLE

As you read through the chapter, you probably figured out pretty easily who in your relationship is the Turtle and who is the Hailstorm. If not, think about how you respond when you're really frustrated. If you're still stumped, you can ask your partner!

Coaxing That Turtle Out

You're a Hailstorm and your Turtle is firmly stuck in their shell. Here are some ideas for luring them out:

1. Ask them what they need right now. *Don't get upset if they aren't sure. Just ask the question, and then focus on being someone your partner feels safe confiding in. Become more curious about why your Turtle has a hard shell (and a soft belly).*

2. Don't do anything. *This is the simplest (and generally most effective) option. But it's also often the hardest for a Hailstorm. The thing is, if you give your Turtle a bit of space, they will peek out of their shell before you know it—and you won't feel like you're in it alone anymore.*

3. Write a short, kind note of sincere praise, and leave it somewhere for them to find (e.g. on their desk, nightstand, in their briefcase, taped to the bathroom mirror). *This reminds the Turtle that they are appreciated.*

Calming the Hailstorm Down

You're a Turtle, and your Hailstorm is at full fury, pounding you with their golf-ball-sized hail. Here are some ideas to soothe the storm cloud away:

1. Leave them a token of appreciation—a flower, a kind note, or a favorite snack. *This little gesture lets them know you care about them, and that you're not withdrawing.*

2. Ask, "What's going on?" Listen, and repeat back what your Hailstorm says.

3. If you really want to calm the Hailstorm, you can ask: "Is there something I can do for you?" *More than anything, this will let the Hailstorm know that you've got their back. And having a partner who has their back means everything to the Hailstorm. The thing is, you've got to follow up and actually DO whatever it is that they've said you could do for them. Otherwise you can expect the hail you're receiving to get even bigger!*

And Remember:

Incompatibility is not only grounds for marriage. . . .
It's the opportunity to create a great marriage!

Conflict Is Growth Trying to Happen

HARVILLE

Hopefully by now you realize that the conflict you're experiencing is not only normal, but inevitable and even *valuable*. Don't try to avoid it. Don't try to deny it. Don't run away from it, or wish it away. Stay with it, and you'll discover something wonderful right around the corner.

While conflict makes you uncomfortable, it can also invite you to reflect on your situation from a new perspective. So you have a choice. You can act in ways that keep the conflict going. Or you can turn the conflict into creative tension, which gives birth to new insights and talents.

In fact, **conflict is growth trying to happen**.

All of us want Real Love. It's what we thought we were signing up for when we said "I do." And we were. But there are two necessary pit stops on the journey:

1. Romantic Love: Now this stop is pure ecstasy! Pleasure chemicals are released into your brain, bonding you to your partner. It feels great. You'd happily stay here forever.

2. Power Struggle: Unfortunately, every couple ends up here. You see all your partner's negative qualities, which suck the pleasure chemicals in your brain dry. Feeling lost, it seems like you're going down, down, DOWN!

Survive these two pit stops, and you're well on your way. Real Love is the harmonious intimacy you hoped for, the communion created from a relationship built on mutual caring and respect. Like anything worth having, getting to Real Love is a process. The journey is quite an adventure, and our book is a terrific road map.

We highlight these pit stops because so many conflicted couples believe there is something wrong with their relationship. There is a myth in our culture: **If you're having problems in your marriage, it means you're with the wrong person.** *This is not true.*

Sadly, the pain and confusion of the Power Struggle cause many couples to consider bailing. They love the romance, but assume that the Power Struggle means it's time to take the Exit Ramp. Some get divorced. Others stay together, living parallel lives. The ones who bail think they're lucky. But any new relationship journey begins with Romantic Love.

Which means the Power Struggle is right around the corner.

No one escapes this! The new love interest may look, talk,

laugh, and/or act differently than your current partner. But once Romantic Love fades, watch out. They will morph into an eerie replica of the partner that was left behind.

Bailing during the Power Struggle stops something beautiful that is struggling to be born into the relationship. You'll be getting rid of your partner, but keeping the problem. Better to keep the partner and get rid of the problem. How? By getting curious about what the conflict is trying to give birth to in your relationship.

STOPPING THE CYCLE

Couples in our workshops feel *such relief* when we explain that every couple gets locked in the Power Struggle. They realize they aren't alone! The trick is to **use conflict to jump-start growth.**

Sadly, Helen and I were just like our workshop couples. We were absolutely deadlocked in the Power Struggle. Here's a bit of how it looked, and how we eventually found the Promised Land on the other side.

When my mother died I was too stunned to cry, at first. At

the funeral, my family complimented me for holding it all in. One of my older sisters admiringly called me "little man." Remember, I was only six. When the shock of my mother's death wore off, I was ready for tears. But I'd absorbed the powerful message from the adults around me that expressing feelings was *not* okay. As a result, I buried my feelings deep inside. This caused me to relate in life through my intellect. I committed myself to developing outstanding communication skills, logically writing and speaking my thoughts.

My emotions were so deeply buried that sometimes *I didn't even know how I felt.* This frustrated Helen, especially when she wanted to work on Imago childhood exercises together. Looking into my blank face, she felt like she was married to a robot.

By contrast, Helen's family gave her permission to feel, laugh, play, sing, dance—even cry. Remember, we're talking the Southern Belle Culture back in the 1970s and 1980s. It was fine for women to express their emotions. But they weren't expected (or even really encouraged) to develop logical, linear skills. And just forget about technical or office skills. Her all-girls school didn't even *teach* typing. When she asked why, they told her she wouldn't need it.

The message was clear: It was okay for Helen to feel—but it wasn't okay for her to take her ideas too seriously, or logically organize her thoughts. So Helen would ramble on in conversations, and talk about her feelings. A lot. And it began to drive me nuts!

About the only thing we agreed on was that I'd cornered the market on "thinking" in the relationship, and Helen on "feeling."

Can you guess what happened next?

When issues arose in our marriage, I'd get increasingly robot-like. Rather than rationally discussing this with me, Helen would unconsciously start carrying the emotions in the relationship for *both* of us. This meant Helen would get *doubly* emotional. I'd get so frustrated! I'd eventually snap and become hypercritical.

All I wanted was for Helen to think more logically (so *I* wouldn't have to deal with the chaos of her feelings).

All Helen wanted was for me to feel (so I'd be able to empathize with *her* feelings).

Unfortunately, the more critical I became, the less articulate Helen got. And I'd become even more critical. You see the picture? So how did we get out of this mess?

This is where our conflict—when used as creative tension— helped us grow something new in our relationship.

The fact is that my ability to feel deeply was simply lost to me. And Helen's ability to think and speak logically was undeveloped. What we came to realize was that **the part of your partner that drives you the *craziest* is often the part you secretly long to be**

more like. Once we recognized this, the real work began. We wound up giving birth to whole new parts of ourselves!

My task was to give myself permission to feel. This was terrifying. It meant experiencing what the loss of my mother had *really* felt like for my six-year-old self. It's a place I'd avoided for decades. I'm a guy who likes control and order, and I wasn't exactly keen on having to go there. Who would be?

The thing is, I could feel myself shutting down whenever Helen needed me to show up emotionally for her. She'd remind me that in order to get out of this mess, I needed to consider my childhood wounding. Boy, did I resist that idea! The more I resisted, the more our conflict grew. Finally, I gathered up my courage and dove into my grief, feeling and sorting through all the other emotions I'd pushed down along the way. And was it ever messy!

Thank goodness Helen wasn't afraid of the chaos that came as I learned how to express deep feelings. She knew I could do it, and her confidence in my abilities was so important to me— because I wasn't feeling confident at all. Lifted up by her faith in me, I explored this new emotional terrain.

The more I went for it, the greater the gifts. Helen told me how connecting my heart and brain actually deepened my wisdom and understanding. And though diving into my feelings was challenging at first, I wound up gaining so much! Here I was, the scholarly robot, suddenly tearing up at a sunset and crying when someone did something caring for me. It was and continues to be amazing to really let in these meaningful life moments.

Also, the more comfortable I was with my own feelings, the easier it was to be with others who were experiencing emotions. I'd always been able to do this well with the couples I counseled. But it had been harder to bring that same openness to Helen and our family. Not anymore!

Helen's task was to start expressing herself in a more organized way. One day she came to me with an insight: "I want a computer!" Ever ready to be logical (okay, yes, *and* critical), I said, "What on earth for? You can't type!" (How's that for sensitivity?) Refusing to give up, Helen said, "Well, I can teach myself." And she marched out of the room.

The next day, Helen came home with a laptop. She looked both triumphant and very shy. To be honest, I was a bit shocked, but also absolutely thrilled. And I wanted to support her in whatever way I could. I immediately helped Helen set up her new laptop, and found her a computer program to learn typing. Neither one of us knew quite what we were unleashing.

After three or four months, Helen was just going to town on her new computer. One day, hearing the astonishingly fast clicking of the keys, I asked her what she was typing. "I've never told you this before, Harville," she said, "but I think there's a book inside me. My mother wanted to write a book, but she never got it finished. I don't know if I will either, but I've got to try." I was intrigued.

Helen had been invaluable helping me develop Imago theory and advising me on my writing. Now, here I was able to help her make her thoughts more logical and linear on paper. I loved doing this! And I never doubted that she'd finish. When her book was published, we were both so proud.

Often what we need most from our partner is what they are least capable of giving (which also means that we're the least capable of giving them what they most need from us). Sadly, adults can find it hard to learn new skills. Learning something new takes courage.

So get ready for some serious s-t-r-e-t-c-h-i-n-g.

It won't look pretty (at first). And it certainly won't feel comfortable.

This is why we call it the Stretching Principle.

Because growth requires both partners to stretch into new ways of being. It's about using emotional muscles that we haven't used before.

The Stretching Principle.

I worked on feeling. And Helen worked on thinking and talking logically. Each week we'd stretch a little bit more. I cannot tell you how hard this was for both of us. But, bit-by-bit, we made progress (and still are, by the way). The more we stick with it, the easier it becomes. And the more amazing it feels.

What began as a HUGE conflict resulted in our giving birth to profound parts of ourselves:

- My growth empowered me to be present for my loved ones and the world in a way I'd barely allowed myself to dream of before. It also connected me to the young, trusting self who had not yet experienced the grief of my parents' deaths. This allowed me to find my heart. Suddenly, I could lecture and write with both my heart and mind.

- Helen's growth empowered her to go back to school, earn her Ph.D., write articles, and become a published author. All of this meant learning how to think and speak logically, which she does beautifully now. As much as writing her book was important to Helen for her own sake, she hoped it could also be a gift to her mother in some way. Helen cannot share this story without tears coming to her eyes.

Many people feel that Romantic Love fades far too fast. And for some, the conflict of the Power Struggle lasts way too long. Remember, though, that there is a purpose to the struggle. To move through it, you have to recognize the **real message behind the conflict: It's time for both you and your partner to stretch so you can reclaim new parts of yourself.** Using the conflict as a catalyst enables you to truly become the partner each one of you needs, and also develop fully into all of who you are.

Truth #3: Conflict Is Growth Trying to Happen

EXERCISE: MISSES AND WISHES

First:

1. Write down the things you loved about your relationship when you first met, and miss now (See "Misses and Wishes" on page 162).

2. Next write down something you've been longing to feel in your relationship—something you've possibly never felt before.

Then:

Take turns sharing items from each list. As you do, it's natural for memories to come up. Share those too. For example, if one of your wishes is that you'd love to travel more often, this might lead you to a memory of a wonderful trip you took together early in your relationship. Sharing that memory—and even cuddling while you do it—will get your brain to release the love hormone oxytocin, which is responsible for the wonderful feelings you had when you were in the Romantic Love phase of your relationship.

You can also make a list of things you want to create in your relationship and hang it on the fridge. Some of these may be relatively small (like being more affectionate with each other or having friends over more), and some might be larger (like going on a second honeymoon). Having your relationship wishes in plain sight will remind you to focus on creating them.

And Remember:

By stretching to give your partner what they need, you grow new skills.

Being Present for Each Other Heals the Past

HELEN

Now, finally (drum roll, please), we get to the heart of what seems to be part of the universal mystery. There is an amazing thing that happens when we transform the energy of conflict into growth, allowing us to answer the true calling of committed partnership. **You become your partner's healer—and they become yours.** As you start listening to your partner in a new way, you will realize an important fact: **Your partner's needs are a blueprint for your own healing and growth—and your needs are a blueprint for your partner's.**

There is an old kind of marriage. In it, both people are elbow-ing each other, trying to get into the center. Each one expects the other to put the attention on *them* and *meet their needs*. This kind of marriage doesn't work. Today, a new kind of marriage is emerging: the Partnership Marriage. This marriage isn't about you . . . or even your partner. The Partnership Marriage is about something that is greater than either one of you. It is about the two of you helping each other grow into full adulthood. And the healing of each other's childhood wounds is at the heart of this process.

GIVING YOU WHAT YOU NEED HEALS ME

Identifying each other's blueprint to healing is like a four-step dance. You and your partner must: (1) help each other name your wounds; (2) clarify what you both need to heal; (3) grow your-selves into becoming each other's healer (by stretching to meet each other's needs); and (4) become stronger and more complete in the process.

I made a big mistake with the first two steps of this dance. Remember how proud I was that I "knew Harville better than he knew himself"? That meant I kept giving him the WRONG things to heal his wounds. One day I realized: Rather than as-suming I knew what he needed, I had to *ask* him. Now the first few times I asked my Turtle-husband what he needed, he said he didn't know. This wasn't Harville being difficult. This was the Turtle not feeling safe enough to come out of his shell and tell me.

So I didn't press. Instead *I focused on fully accepting his answer and being safe for him*—so that in time, he might feel like sharing. Eventually Harville's defenses relaxed and he was able to identify and share what he needed. Harville explained that he didn't want me to prepare food for him before he even knew if he was hungry or lay out his clothes for him in the morning. He wanted me to be emotionally *present* for him. To *listen* to him.

The idea of "being present" may sound easy to you. It means giving all of your attention to your partner in a caring, open-hearted way—really listening to what your partner thinks and feels. Just because someone is in the same room with you, or is even looking right at you, doesn't mean they are present with you.

Truly being present for someone is a real gift. And boy was it hard for me. When I was little, neither of my parents had been present for me. Becoming present for Harville meant I had to slow down and be available to hear more of his thoughts.

Remember how Harville admitted that learning to be a Hailstorm was messy? Here's how it progressed: I was nagging Harville a little bit about being a robot. (Okay, a LOT!) I realized *that* approach wasn't getting us anywhere. So I slowed down. Instead of ACTING and DOING constantly, I worked on developing deeper inner peace and quiet within myself.

Then TA-DA, one day Harville popped out of his shell. He began to express his feelings like I'd asked him to. But to my surprise (and horror!) the feelings were anger and resentment. "Whoa!" I thought. "Maybe asking him to feel wasn't such a good idea after all. . . ."

Then I remembered that the majority of Harville's anger had to do with his childhood. This calmed me down enough to simply accept his feelings. My growth, I knew, was about learning to stay steady (like a Turtle). I had to be safe, strong, and calm in his presence—even when he was upset.

Pretty soon, Harville's anger melted away. In its place came gratitude—that I was willing to be present with *all* of his feelings without getting defensive. Soon after, Harville's loving feelings bubbled up and out. (Blush, blush!) Our relationship went from being terribly strained to feeling wonderful. It was miraculous!

Because of my childhood wounding, I'd been on autopilot my whole life, "*doing* for others." It was EXHAUSTING. Still, it was hard to stop "doing" and just listen. But the more I focused on listening better and learning to be present for Harville, the easier it felt. And it turned out to be *much* easier than figuring out what he wanted and doing things for him before he even asked. Whew! Now I could relax.

And something else miraculous happened as well.

In learning to become present for Harville, I began to be more present for my own feelings. The whole setup of creating Real Love required that I become more self-aware.

It turns out Harville and I had the exact same wound: abandonment. Neither one of us had a primary caregiver who was truly present for us when we were children. We just expressed our wounds in opposite ways. Harville buried his feelings, which made it hard for him to be emotionally present. And I spread myself thin, trying to be emotionally present for everyone.

This is the crux and calling of a truly committed and conscious partnership: We need to answer the call to become each other's healers. It means that you avoid, at all cost, re-wounding each other—so that you can become true advocates for each other. Only for the strong-willed, this is an art—an honor—a Sacred Duty.

CREATING SAFE SPACE

The key to this transformation happening is safety. By safety, we mean two people living in relationship with neither feeling hurt, criticized, or put down by the other. When your partner doesn't feel safe, they put up their defenses. When this happens, you may think you've been living with your partner, but you've actually been living with their *defenses*. If you can help your partner feel safe, they will soon drop their defenses to come out and play! Only then can they do the work they need to do.

This is why safety is a thread running throughout this book. **Healing happens only in a safe environment.** Without safety, healing won't happen.

So how do you achieve safety? Consider the following. . . .

The common way of thinking about relationships goes something like this: When a relationship is in trouble, it's assumed that one or both of the people need "fixing." So they go to a therapist. Or they buy books about fixing one or the other (and it's usually the *other*). The belief is that each individual in the partnership has to get healthy in order to create a healthy relationship.

Harville and I flipped that idea on its head. We believe that if a relationship is in trouble, the couple needs to focus on *healing the relationship*. *Not* on themselves. In fact, Harville and I would assert that **the best way to heal a relationship is not to repair the two people, but the Space Between them.** Hmmm, interesting . . .

THE "SPACE BETWEEN"

So what is this Space Between? The moment you committed to each other, it was born. You can think of it as an energy field filling up the space between you two.

Right now, we're imagining you might have the same kind of look on your face that we get from couples in our workshops. Many are suspicious. Others think we're off our rockers! And many insist: "There isn't anything between me and my partner but . . . well, AIR."

It may look like there isn't anything between you. But there is.

Consider outer space. Our universe is filled with stars, planets, meteors, and comets. What lies between all these cosmic bodies? Space. Lots of space. Lots of EMPTY space. Right?

Wrong.

We used to think space was empty. But astronomers have proven that the space between the planets isn't empty at all. It is filled with gravitational pull and energy fields that actually hold the planets in their orbits.

And so it is with the Space Between. It is a cosmic energy field that supports you both in your relationship. Just as physics is part of the physical world, we believe there is a physics that governs the Space Between you and your partner.

THE PHYSICS OF THE SPACE BETWEEN

Every word, tone of voice, every glance, affects the Space Between. Even the unspoken communication of your body language (called nonverbal cues) contributes to this energy field.

There are times when you and your partner feel accepted by each other. The air is safe to breathe. These are the times when the Between is filled with love.

Then there are times when things are strained. The air is thick with judgment. Tension coils all around you. These are the times when the Between is filled with conflict. The state of the Between determines how safe you and your partner feel in each other's presence. So we're going to give you, as my yoga instructor says, a "mantra"—a statement that we want you to repeat over and over again. Tape it to every mirror in your house. Say it ten times throughout the day.

Ready for the mantra?

Here it is: **NO shame, blame, or criticism in our Between!**

Criticism, blame, and shame are like toxins. They act as acid on the Between, corroding your connection to your partner. Your goal is to make the Between safe. This means loving and empathizing with each other through it all. Yes, we mean ALL! Your partner's fun and happy feelings, *and* their not so fun ones. It was amazing when Harville learned to do this for me.

All my life I'd been given the message that only those who were sweet and nice were worthy of love. Then I hit a period when stress turned me into a real grouch. And Harville really stepped up. Instead of criticizing my behavior, he became a steady, loving presence for me. It was simply wonderful.

One day, I woke up and suddenly SAW myself and realized: "I have so many ways I should be working on myself to become a more loving person. That should be my focus!" I would not have made it to this liberated place if Harville had been critical of me. It was his loving presence that made it safe for me to see how I was really being. When two people make the Space Between truly Sacred Space, that's when the healing can happen.

By Sacred Space, we mean space that is absolutely holy. The Between may look like ordinary air. But don't *ever* treat it in an ordinary way. Your relationship needs to be the most important thing in the world to you. Never, never, never violate the Space Between with anything that will hurt your relationship. Truly think of it as holy ground.

This is the act of building Real Love. It leads to a genuine homecoming. One built on a solid foundation of trust and caring.

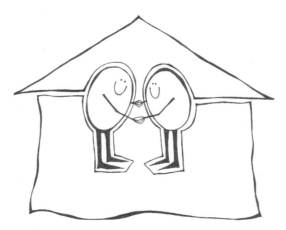

The Genuine Homecoming of Real Love.

And none of this would be possible if we were not bound with someone who re-wounds us like our parents did!

We were all wounded in relationship. *We can heal only in relationship.* This is why we have to answer the call to become each other's healers.

And it all hinges on what you choose to put into the Space Between.

Truth #4: Being Present for Each Other Heals the Past

EXERCISE: "SPRING CLEANING" FOR THE BETWEEN

First:

1. In the pictures on pages 168–169, write your name in one of the small circles and your partner's name in the other.

2. In the large circle at the top, list as many thoughts, feelings, and behaviors as you can that describe the positive things in your Between, the things that are WONDERFUL. These are the things that bring safety, connection, and/or passion into your relationship, like: respect, love, co-parenting, date nights.

3. In the circle at the bottom, list as many thoughts, feelings, and behaviors as you can that describe the negative things in your Between, the things that are CHALLENGING. These are the things that bring doubt, disconnection, and/or upset into your relationship, like: distrust, criticizing, lack of intimacy, no fun.

Then:

Share with your partner how *they* contribute to what is *wonderful* in your relationship. *(For example: "The best thing I see you bring to our space is . . .")* Follow that up with how *you* contribute to the challenges. *(For example: "I feel I contribute to our challenges when I . . .")* Finally, explore some ideas together on how you both can increase the wonderful

and remove the challenges so that you create safety in the
Between, transforming it into Sacred Space.

And Remember:
One of the most beautiful and profound things
about relationship is that we're called into the role
of being each other's healer.
This means NO shame, blame, or criticism in your Between!

It's Not WHAT You Say; It's HOW You Say It

HELEN

Before we can take on all this healing, however, we HAVE to learn a new way to talk. What's the old way? It's what humans have been doing since the dawn of time. It's called monologue: where one person at a time is talking but no one is really listening.

When couples do it, it's called parallel monologue. Two people talking. No one listening.

When Harville and I met, our communication was a supreme example of parallel monologues! We shared many common interests. Our courtship was full of passionate conversation. Much was exciting. But we also had impassioned disagreements. We are both bullheaded. We both love to debate. And we found ourselves both talking at the same time—especially if we disagreed about something. Over time, this became very frustrating for us.

One day I finally said to Harville, "Could we please take turns?"

He looked shocked, but then replied, "Well, sure, I guess so . . ."

The result? We co-created what came to be called the Imago Dialogue Process. You've got to love a guy who responds to a simple request by creating a revolutionary new way to communicate!

I realized early on that there were some very positive reasons for dating a relationship therapist!

As far as the subject of talking goes, our culture rewards those who speak up. Almost every school has a debate club. Compliments are given to those who can clearly and persuasively speak their mind. The majority of those who get promoted in life are those who express themselves well.

If we are feeling disturbed about something, we're told we should talk about it. Psychology was, in fact, originally called "the talking cure." And, in a sense, the root of healing involves two people talking. What most people leave out is that HOW you talk is really important. They also leave out one other little detail. When one of you is talking, the other one has to REALLY LISTEN.

Our culture does not reward people for listening. So, even during the best of times, our listening skills are pretty rusty. And during the worst—like when we're locked in the Power Struggle— forget it! It becomes all about who can demand what they want the loudest (Hailstorm) and/or who can shut down and freeze out their partner the longest (Turtle).

During the Power Struggle, listening just flies out the window.

Dialogue changes all that. The Power Struggle ruptures connection. Dialogue sustains and deepens connection. **Dialogue is** a structured way of talking and listening that builds connection between you and your partner. It is this connection that enables you to heal your childhood wounds. It may feel clumsy at first. But, the process supports you and your partner as you identify each other's needs and learn how to honor them.

You were taught the key to Dialogue in kindergarten: (1) take turns, and (2) don't interrupt. One of you talks while the other listens. Then you switch. This sounds simple. But it's so different from what most people do that it's important to practice.

Dialogue has three steps: Mirroring, Validating, and Empathizing. Before you begin, you and your partner should decide who will be the Sender (the one speaking) and who will be the Receiver (the one listening). Because the Sender wants the Receiver's full attention, we suggest you ask for an appointment by saying: "Are you available to do the Dialogue Process?"

We know it feels stiff and a little weird to talk this way to your partner. But there is a reason we suggest using these exact words. As both you and your partner become more comfortable with Dialogue, this question alone will "cue" your partner to become grounded and intentional (that is, ready for Dialogue).

When you ask your partner for an Imago Dialogue, they can say no if the timing isn't good for them. But they have to follow up their "not now" with a suggested alternative time.

If the Receiver feels ready in that moment, they will say yes. By "ready" we mean the Receiver feels like they can bring thoughtfulness and care to what the Sender is saying.

It is from this respectful place that you both begin Dialogue.

To learn the Dialogue Process we suggest you and your partner start by sharing what you appreciate about each other. We call this "Giving Appreciations." Doing this has been magical for us. We give them to each other every day, and encourage you to do the same. Once you both feel comfortable using Dialogue with Appreciations, you will be ready to use the process for more difficult issues. An explanation of the three steps follows.

STEP ONE: MIRRORING

The Sender starts by sending a message. And they do it with **Sender Responsibility**. That is, the Sender should send their message clearly and kindly. Doing so increases the chance their partner will hear it. The Receiver then Mirrors, that is, repeats back, what they heard—using the Sender's exact words.

For example, if the Sender says: "Hey, I want to share something you did recently that I really appreciated. You arrived at our date last Friday night right on time. That meant a lot to me—it made me feel as though our time together was really important to you." The Receiver would respond: "**Let me see if I got it.** I did something you appreciated. I arrived at our date last Friday night right on time. This meant a lot to you, and made you feel as though our time together was really important to me. **Did I get it?**"

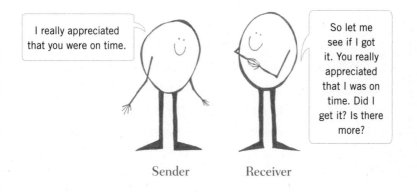

> I really appreciated that you were on time.

> So let me see if I got it. You really appreciated that I was on time. Did I get it? Is there more?

Sender   Receiver

"**Let me see if I got it.**" and "**Did I get it?**" are key phrases. You want to make sure you are very clear about what your partner said. Don't edit their words. Don't respond with your own reactions. Even if they do say something wrong—for example, you actually went out Saturday night instead of Friday—*let it go*. These kinds of specifics don't matter. Your first job is to make the Sender feel that their words are accepted by you.

If this feels awkward at first, don't worry. You're in good company. A lot of people experience the same thing early on. After some practice, though, a beautiful thing happens. Your partner will feel deeply touched when they experience you reflecting back their words.

After the Sender confirms that the Receiver Mirrored accurately, the Receiver asks, "**Is there more?**" Your partner will be amazed! They've probably never heard this question before. Instead, for most of their life, they've heard something more like: "Are you done yet?"

So the Receiver asks the magical question: "Is there more?" And the Sender might respond with something like: "Well, yes, I just want you to understand how much this touches me. Both my parents were so busy when I was growing up. And when they did attend an event that was special to me, they were often late. I could never count on them. I'd be so disappointed. I know you're busy. We both are. I do my best to protect our special time together, and I really appreciate it when you do too. It makes me feel loved, instead of disappointed like I was when I was a kid."

Be sure you use the phrase "**Is there more?**" It truly is an enchanted grouping of words. It shows that you're curious. And makes your partner feel safe. The safer they feel, the more willing they will be to share much deeper things with you. Once the

Sender shares, the Receiver Mirrors the Sender's response to "Is there more?"

When the Sender says that they feel Mirrored, congratulations! You've made it through step one of the Imago Dialogue Process.

STEP TWO: VALIDATING

The Receiver now Validates the Sender's words. Validating means that you "get" your partner's point of view. The Receiver does so by sincerely saying: **"You make sense."**

This doesn't mean you, as the Receiver, necessarily agree with what your partner said (though you might). *Agreement is not the goal.* Everyone makes sense from their own perspective. It's just that everyone is coming from a different perspective! And when you take time to see things from your partner's point of view, you will see that *they do make sense.*

This is an important step. The words can't be said mechanically. The Sender has to really feel that you, the Receiver, are being genuine when you say, "You make sense." When you as the Receiver Validate your partner, you're giving your partner the message that: "you have a right to feel and think the way you do." Given that you're actually married to **another person**, your partner *does* have that right!

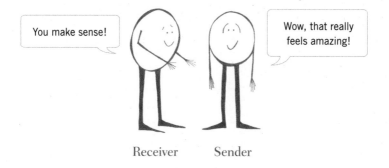

You make sense!

Wow, that really feels amazing!

Receiver   Sender

The great thing is that your partner will soon be in the Receiver's seat. This means they'll be entering *your* world, Mirroring, Validating, and Empathizing with *your* point of view!

Most of us believe that our way is the Right Way—and we're willing to fight this to the death! The problem is that this approach *is* a death—it kills your connection to your partner. We regularly ask couples, "Do you want to be right, or do you want to be in relationship?" Because you can't always have both. You can't cuddle up and relax with "being right" after a long day.

STEP THREE: EMPATHIZING

Now it's time for the Receiver to Empathize with the Sender by suggesting a word or two that they think would describe the Sender's emotional state. When doing this, remember that there are four core feelings: glad, mad, sad, and scared. All other feelings are varieties of these, so you don't have to get fancy and consult a thesaurus. Just suggest a simple feeling. Then ask your partner if you got their feelings right.

For example, the Receiver might say: "Given how disappointed you were that your parents were often late when you were little, I can imagine you might be feeling glad when I'm on time, and you appreciate me. Is that what you're feeling?" And if the Receiver got it right, the Sender would say: "Yes, that's it exactly!"

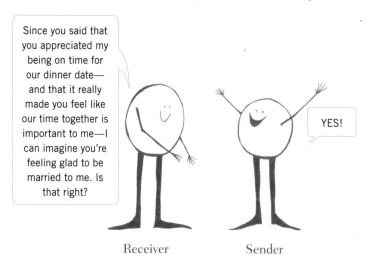

Receiver   Sender

Are you beginning to see how it works? The issue to remember is: **Each of you has wounds from childhood, . . . and the purpose of marriage is to heal those wounds.**

Through Dialogue, we become aware of painful memories and feelings that have been buried deep inside us. Re-experiencing them with a loving partner who can listen and empathize helps us to heal. It makes such a difference when we experience ourselves being listened to with empathy rather than judgment.

BUT WHO HAS THE TIME?

Dialogue can feel a bit stiff and formal at first. It can also feel like it's taking a long time.

The thing is, Dialogue isn't supposed to be quick. To discover who our partner really is, and the ways we ourselves were wounded, we have to slow down. The whole point of Dialogue, in fact, is that it *slows you down*.

Dialogue may even feel frustrating at first. Because you'll be trying to explain to your partner how *you* feel. And listening to how *they* feel. And trying to figure out *what* your needs are. But in the midst of struggling to get the steps right, it's like a door swings open in your relationship. It can feel like sunshine breaking through the clouds. Your fears diminish and you begin to feel connected. You get to the point where you may completely disagree with something your partner thinks or feels. But from this open, empathic place, you grow to understand it—and them—more deeply. You begin to experience your relationship as wondrous and deeply fulfilling.

And if this isn't enough of an incentive to stick with Dialogue, think of the alternative. How long does it take to have an argument? And then recover from it?

Compared to that, Dialogue actually takes no time at all!

So you decide how you want to spend time with your partner. Arguing or in Dialogue.

Mirroring is about establishing contact with your partner. Validating creates connection. And Empathizing moves you into communion. This is the act of transforming your relationship into a Sacred Space.

Truth #5: It's Not WHAT You Say; It's HOW You Say It

EXERCISE: THE IMAGO DIALOGUE PROCESS

First:

1. Choose who will be the Sender and who will be the Receiver.

2. Pick a topic. We suggest you start with something positive like sharing an Appreciation about your partner or sharing something about your day at work.

3. To begin, the Sender asks the Receiver for an appointment by saying: "Are you available for an Imago Dialogue?"

    And go to www.MakingMarriageSimple.com *for video examples and other resources.*

Step One: Mirroring

The Sender states their message, using Sender Responsibility.

The Receiver reflects back ONLY what the Sender says using the following language: "So let me see if I got it. You *[insert here exactly what your partner said]*. Did I get it?"

After the Sender confirms that the Receiver got it, the Receiver asks: "Is there more?"

The Receiver continues Mirroring until the Sender feels fully heard.

Step Two: Validating

The Receiver Validates the Sender's point of view by simply acknowledging: "You make sense." And remember, agreement is not the goal.

Step Three: Empathizing

As the Receiver, try to relate to the feelings underneath the issue the Sender shared. Remember, there are four core feelings: mad, sad, glad, and scared.

So to Empathize, the Receiver says something like: "Given that *[insert once again what your partner said regarding the issue]*, I can imagine you might be feeling *[use a word or two that might describe your partner's emotional state]*."

Then check in with "Is that what you're feeling?"

If the Sender says: "No, I'm really feeling X," then the Receiver Mirrors what the Sender said.

Once the Sender responds positively that the Receiver got how they feel, you can switch. The Sender becomes the Receiver and the Receiver becomes the Sender.

The key to Dialogue is practice, practice, practice!

Then:

Continue practicing Dialogue. We suggest you set aside time for full Dialogues, *and* you can also practice randomly throughout the day. It helps train the brain! For example:

- "If I heard you correctly, you said pass the salt. Did I get it?" (Mirroring)
- "Is there more about that?"

- "So you just said you would rather I not make a mess right after you've worked hard to clean the kitchen. That makes sense." (Validating)
- "Wow, your boss said that to you? I can imagine this made you feel really happy and proud. Did I get it?" (Empathizing)

Every interaction is an opportunity to bring Dialogue into your lives. Have fun with it!

And Remember:

In Dialogue, agreement is not the goal.
The goal is to take turns and really listen to each other.

TRUTH #6

Negativity Is Invisible Abuse

HELEN

The thing is, however, the kind of communion we're talking about can't happen in a relationship that's full of negativity.

During the time when our marriage teetered between renewal and divorce, Harville and I were visiting a bookstore. On a whim, we picked up an astrology book on relationships. Turning to the page that explained how our two birth dates intersected, we read: **"You will destroy your relationship unless you end your negative scrutiny of each other."** We were stunned. *How* did the author know us so well?

The truth of that statement cut to the heart of our problem. And we didn't even have to pay for a therapist!

Our definition of **negativity is any words, tone of voice, facial expression** (such as rolling your eyes), **or behavior your partner says feels negative to them.**

Our partner decides when we're being negative.

Yes, your partner decides if you're being negative or not. You might say you're only joking. But if it doesn't feel good to your partner, you need to CUT IT OUT. Negativity makes your partner feel unsafe. Without safety in your relationship, your partner will never grow. And your relationship will never be transformed.

Harville and I found three key ways we unknowingly slipped into negativity, and we soon discovered these were the same ways couples in our workshops did too. They are: (1) critical thinking, (2) competition, and (3) oh dear, heaven forbid, "constructive criticism."

CRITICAL THINKING

Critical thinking helps us in many ways. It's what we use to make sure we walk out the door in matching socks. It reminds us to check for any toilet paper stuck to our shoe before leaving the bathroom. Who wouldn't want to be thinking critically while driving? It helps us anticipate what other drivers might do. Without it, who knows how many accidents we'd get into?

In our society we're even REWARDED for critical thinking. Teachers love students who critique their papers before turning them in. Harville and I know this well—because we're both trained academics. Bosses love employees who think critically because it helps them identify ways something can be improved. Engage in some critical thinking at work, and watch how it appears under "strengths" on your performance review.

Critical thinking has its place—but that place is NOT in your marriage. We're generally the most critical of our partner when they aren't acting or reacting to things the way *we* think they *should*.

And this annihilates your partner.

So in our workshops, we tell our couples: Your partner is NOT you.

Because when you're critical about how your partner acts or reacts, **you're really getting upset at them for not being you**.

When I felt really emotional, Harville would get really critical of how hard it was for me to clearly explain my feelings. Put simply, he'd get upset that I was upset. And he'd give me pointers on how I could bullet out my feelings—so that I could be more linear and concise in my communication. He'd do this *right in the middle of my feeling so upset*. The last thing I needed in that moment was a communication coach.

He came to realize that he was getting upset with me for not being more Turtle-like (i.e., more like *him*). Couples do this to each other all the time.

To end this scenario of mutual destruction, you have to accept that you are two different people, with different preferences and different ways of doing things. Unfortunately, having differences makes it easy to slip into . . .

COMPETITION

On the surface, Harville and I seem very easygoing and relaxed. But scratch the surface even the tiniest bit, and you'll discover the deep, dark truth: We are both stubborn mules! Honestly, I don't think you could find a more hardheaded, competitive pair than the two of us.

In our defense, let's face it: It's human nature to compete. In our culture whoever talks the most convincingly or gets their way is the "Top Dog." To win this game, all of us are taught to insist on our rights and debate our point better than the next person.

Competition has its place—but that place is NOT smack-dab in the middle of your marriage.

The obvious way couples are competitive is when each one asserts that they are "right" (read: superior) and the other is "wrong" (read: inferior).

But here's an interesting little twist on competition that most don't think about. . . .

You can be competitive about who is the *worst* too.

How would this look? Of course Harville and I have an example!

After the two of us figured out how much our childhood wounding plays a role in our adult lives and relationships, guess what we did? Yep! We started competing to determine which of us had a rougher time. Can you believe it?

There we'd be, delving into the big and little traumas from our childhoods, each of us trying to prove that WE had more to overcome." And let me caution you about something right now: Don't try to engage in this game with someone who lost his or her parents at a young age. Because, honestly, there isn't much that can top that.

Luckily Harville and I figured out a long time ago that when Romantic Love snares two people in its net, it makes sure it chooses two people who've got about the same amount of work to do. Which means you and your partner are wounded at the same level. So you can end the competition about who had it the worst, and focus on helping each other heal.

The bottom line is this: When you feel superior to your partner (whether it is because you believe you're better OR because you feel they didn't have it as bad as you did) this is a sure sign you're in competition.

CONSTRUCTIVE CRITICISM

I bet you're wondering how in the world "constructive criticism" qualifies as being negative. You may feel: "My partner needs my HELP, my **penetrating insights**." I'm sad to admit that I used to feel that way. In the early years of our marriage, one of my favorite pastimes was to offer Harville my "helpful" constructive criticism.

Of course I wanted to be as clear and thorough as possible. That meant getting every little detail right. So I made lists. If he chose a shirt color that made him look washed out, it went on the list. If he forgot to do something around the house, on the list it went. Spinach between his teeth? On the list. If he was being stubborn about something—yep, you guessed it. On. The. List.

Now, please understand, I wasn't *complaining*. I was being HELP-FUL. Who, after all, doesn't want advice so they can become a better person? Plus, I was willing to offer my tidbits of wisdom to

Harville **for free**. Yet despite my "generosity," day-by-day Harville seemed to grow more miserable in our marriage.

The results were pretty awful. While constructive criticism has its place—that place is NOT (you guessed it!) nestled neatly in the loving arms of your marriage.

Let us assure you. There are plenty of people—siblings, bosses, friends, your children, parents—who stand ready and willing to give constructive criticism to your partner. You don't have to be one of them. Your partner is struggling not only with their childhood, but with day-to-day issues. They need an advocate, and that's where you come in.

GOING COLD TURKEY!

The only thing our negativity accomplished was this: Harville and I both felt attacked by each other. And how does one respond when attacked? By putting up one's defenses and counterattacking.

When we realized how destructive this pattern was, we knew we had to cut negativity out of our lives. So we became "negativity watchdogs."

To put it bluntly: **Negativity is invisible abuse and must stop.** After all, no relationship can grow or deepen with negativity.

We admit this is easier said than done. The results from our negativity watch-dogging were disheartening. Harville and I grew to realize that even our briefest conversations contained negativity. I'd share about something going on at work, and Harville would apply his critical thinking, coaching me on how to be more succinct. Enter argument. He'd start to share something with me about some household project he was contemplating. And I'd interrupt him because I already knew how he'd prefer to have it done. Enter argument. Even talking about what to make for dinner wasn't a safe topic! One of us would suggest BBQ chicken and vegetables, and then we'd get into an argument about whether to cook the vegetables (my preferred way) or keep them raw (Harville's preference). It was crazy.

We grew determined to find a cure.

And when we did, we were delighted by its simplicity!

One day, we hung a calendar on our bathroom mirror. At the end of each day, we drew either a smiley face or a frowny face in the space for that day.

A frowny face meant one or both of us had been negative that day. A smiley face meant we both got through the entire day without being negative. Yes, Harville and I—who have four degrees and ten books to our names—had to resort to smiley and frowny faces on a calendar to help break our addiction to negativity. And guess what? It worked!

We were so disgusted by all the frowny faces we saw *day after day,* **week after week**, MONTH after MONTH. S-l-o-w-l-y **all** negative comments ceased.

Yes, *all*. We finally did it!

We were elated by this achievement.

Then a new problem surfaced. . . .

Suddenly, it was SO quiet.

It was embarrassing to admit.

But we didn't know how to speak to each other without being negative. . . .

SHARING APPRECIATION

So we designed another exercise—one that would help us focus on what we actually *liked* about each other. Energy follows attention. We knew that **when we were negative, all we were doing was creating more negativity.** What would happen if we started flooding each other with positive comments?

We found that when we focused on what *was* working, we gradually began to see more and more of the good stuff. To speed up this process, we committed to ending each day by sharing three things we appreciated about each other. Each night we **had** to come up with three **new** things—*no repetitions allowed.*

This was rather challenging, at first.

Our brains weren't in the habit of noticing the positive (and brains in general tend to dwell on the negative). So starting this practice was really awkward. It required us to pay attention to what we *enjoyed* about each other.

Listing our problems had been easy. In contrast, our Appreciations sputtered out. The conversations were filled with uncomfortable pauses.

But we kept at it (proving that being a stubborn mule can, occasionally, be *useful*). And the Appreciations started to come a little bit more easily:

"I appreciated your phone call today, Harville, to check in."

"I appreciated the ideas you offered for my presentation, Helen."

In time, the negative chatter in our minds stopped. And because we were viewing each other from the perspective of all the things we appreciated, we actually began to *see each other differently*. Finally, each of us rediscovered that we were married to an amazing person—something we'd known long ago but had forgotten.

Our **Ritual of Appreciations** created a degree of emotional safety that we'd never experienced before. We fell in love all over again, on a deeper, more wonderful level.

THE WONDER OF IT ALL

We then made another discovery: **The simplest way to turn off negativity is to replace judgment with curiosity.** This one attitude shift has the power to bring wonder back into your relationship.

Why does your partner think the way they do? Feel the way they do? Have you asked them recently?

I thought I knew Harville well. In fact, as you might recall, I thought I knew him *better* than he knew himself. This didn't help our relationship, so I tried shifting from judgment to curiosity. On my list of things I felt judgmental about, Harville's love of *Star Trek* was near the top. I just didn't get it. *Star Trek?* Harville is really smart. I couldn't understand why such a (pardon me, *Star Trek* fans) far-fetched, unrealistic show appealed to him so much.

Then one day I decided to get curious. . . .

So (deep breath) I put my judgment aside. And actually watched a few episodes with him.

First, Harville was absolutely thrilled to have my company on the couch (and cuddling with him was really, really nice!). Then I noticed that *Star Trek* deals with some complex social and cultural ideas. What a surprise! I now fully respect his enjoyment of it—and no longer cringe when he mentions *Star Trek* when we're out with friends. In fact, I've grown to realize that my won-drous husband is similar to Captains James T. Kirk and Jean-Luc Picard. Harville is truly going where no one has gone before. He's out there exploring his own version of "outer space"—the Space Between two people in love.

And all it took was a little curiosity on my part.

Once you try it, you'll be amazed at how easy this shift be-comes.

When you're with your partner, imagine that you're visiting a foreign country. Open yourself up to new ideas and perspectives. Allow yourself to enjoy the different landscape, foods, language, and customs. You don't have to agree with all of your partner's feelings and choices. Just become curious and keep an open mind, so you can discover their unique mystery.

CREATING SAFE SPACE, A REPRISE

Remember our emphasis on safety in Truth #4? **Your job is to be a source of safety for your partner.**

When your partner doesn't feel safe, they put up their de-fenses.

When your partner feels safe, they relax their defenses.

Believe us when we tell you that your partner wants to be a good partner for you. They want to be your hero, or she-ro. We know that each of you genuinely wants the other to be happy. But first you have to stop being negative. Act on this decision, and **everything** will change. And when we say everything, we mean EVERYTHING.

Like many of the ideas in this book, this one shift will pro-foundly impact not only your partnership, but all of your other relationships as well. Eliminate the invisible abuse of negativity with your partner, and it will disappear from your relationships with your children, your friends, and the broader world. People may not realize what's changed, but they'll notice—and **appreciate**—that something's different.

Truth #6: Negativity Is Invisible Abuse
EXERCISE: RITUAL OF APPRECIATIONS

First:

List your partner's physical characteristics, personality traits, behaviors, and global affirmations (e.g., they are terrific, thoughtful, fantastic) that you appreciate, love, admire, and cherish. ("Appreciating You!" on page 176 offers a table and examples.)

Then:

End each day sharing three things you appreciate about each other before going to bed. And commit to doing this Ritual of Appreciations for the remainder of your exercise program—whether you're doing one of the sample programs we offer in the back, or a program that you put together yourself—on the days when you don't have other exercises to do.

Remember, *no repetitions allowed.* You can start with the Appreciations you wrote on your list. But also pay attention to your partner each day from the perspective of what you appreciate about them. The point of this exercise is to shift your focus from what you don't like, to what you do. As your focus shifts, you'll both start seeing more and more of the things you like—and each of you will be inspired to do more for your relationship.

Once you've completed your exercise program, you can even continue giving Appreciations. Why not? It feels great, doesn't it?

And Remember:

Energy follows attention.
The more you focus on the good,
the more good there will be to focus on.

Negativity Is a Wish in Disguise

HARVILLE

Now you may be wondering: Are you supposed to ignore *all* the issues you have with your partner? Let us reassure you. You don't have to passively accept *all* of your partner's sloppy behavior. And we're not suggesting that you just stuff your feelings down.

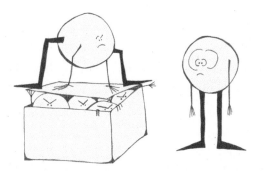

Frustrations? What frustrations?!

Because no matter how successful a stuffer you think you are, the negative feelings won't completely go away.

Instead, you need to recognize that behind every negative thought is an unmet desire.

Negativity is a wish in disguise.

And what is an unmet desire if not a wish?

SAYING IT SO YOUR PARTNER CAN HEAR

Frustrated by your partner's behavior, you want them to change—pronto! But that's only going to happen if they *want* to change. And their willingness to change hinges completely on HOW you bring up issues. **Instead of complaining, you have to state your wish as a request.** And communicate your frustration briefly, using **Sender Responsibility.** As the Sender, **you are responsible for speaking in a way that increases the likelihood that your partner can listen.** Here are some pointers:

1. Use "I" statements ("I feel lonely") not "you" statements ("You're never home"). "You" statements feel like judgments—because they are! "I" statements, on the other hand, invite your partner into how you're feeling.

2. Be brief and clear. Rambling on and on puts you in danger of flooding your partner with more words and emotion than they can handle. Using too many words is a problem for both Turtles and Hailstorms. Flooding your partner makes them feel attacked. They throw up their defenses. Then *you* feel victimized because it seems like they're *never* going to change. What a vicious cycle!

3. You want your partner to respond, so choose only one frustration at a time and state it briefly. If they need more information, trust me, they'll ask.

4. Approach your partner when you're feeling calm. Ask any communication expert and they will tell you that over 90 percent of how someone receives what you say has to do with *how* you communicate it to them. So pay attention to any nonverbal cues you might be displaying, like your

tone of voice, the look in your eye, tapping of your foot, rolling your eyes, sighing, etc.

5. Finally, never criticize, shame, blame, or analyze your partner.

You can flood your partner with too many words. . . .

Using Sender Responsibility is about skillfully inviting your partner to get interested in your wishes. It increases the chance that your partner will want to respond. Be succinct so that your partner can receive what you are saying. Learn how to do this well, and you'll feel like you've acquired a new superpower.

Being able to share frustrations in a way that avoids negativity is so important that we've created a process for it, the Behavior Change Request (BCR). It is another form of the Imago Dialogue Process, with two key additions: You can state your frustration *and* make a request. Like Dialogue, it is simple and straightforward. And, like Dialogue, it can make a profound difference in your relationship.

The BCR is *the* way to state your frustration and keep safety in your relationship all at the same time. It has three simple steps: (1) ask for an appointment to discuss a frustration, (2) state the frustration briefly, and then (3) ask for what you want.

STEP ONE: ASK FOR AN APPOINTMENT

Just like with Dialogue, you don't want to jump into a BCR without checking in first. So always start by asking for an appointment. This could sound like: "I'd love to talk with you about a request I have. Would now be okay?"

Would now be OK?

Yeah, I think I can do it now.

Setting an appointment is important. Your partner may not be in the right state of mind to hear you, and you need to respect that. If now isn't good, let them offer another time. Choosing a time that is good for both of you will help set you *both* up for success.

STEP TWO: BRIEFLY DESCRIBE YOUR FRUSTRATION

When the appointed time comes, the Sender **briefly states their frustration using Sender Responsibility**. Use one sentence if possible—maybe two at the most. For example, the Sender can say: "We've spent the majority of our holidays with your family in recent years, and I miss having special time with my family."

Notice how the statement is brief and to the point. Also notice that the content is about the experience the Sender is having—and not a tirade about how idiotic their partner is for not seeing how unfair the situation is.

The Receiver then Mirrors back exactly what the Sender said: "So let me see if I got it. We've spent the majority of our holidays with my family in recent years, and you miss having special time with your family. Did I get it?" After the Sender confirms that the Receiver got it, the Receiver will ask: **"Is there more?"** The Sender can respond to this question, *but be careful*—stick with something short, sweet, and focused on how the frustration makes *you* feel. Remember: *Don't overload your partner!* The Sender's response might be: "My parents are beginning to get older, and I want us to create good memories with them."

After the Receiver Mirrors this statement, they Validate the Sender's feelings by saying: "It makes sense that you miss having special time with your family." And then they Empathize by saying: "And I can imagine that not having more time with your family might make you feel sad, and that it's unfair. Is that how you're feeling?"

The Sender might respond: "It does feel unfair, and it makes me sad and sometimes even angry." And the Receiver would Validate these feelings, by saying: "Well, your feelings make sense."

STEP THREE: AND NOW THE SMART REQUEST . . .

Now you get to ask for what you want! Once it's clear that your partner has heard you accurately, the next step is to suggest three things your partner could do to ease your frustration. Coming up with three concrete things gives your partner a choice—and they choose one as their gift to you.

When coming up with these requests, we urge you to keep them SMART: Specific, Measurable, Attainable, Relevant, and Time-limited.

"I want to spend every holiday this year with my family instead of yours" may not be attainable. "I want us to spend more time with my family" is not only unspecific, but it can't really be measured. One of your requests might be "I'd like to attend my annual family reunion this year." The time limit creates a due date. Once your partner meets the request, it becomes an obvious place for you to give your partner a gold star for successfully easing your upset!

Making a request is an opportunity to tell your partner *exactly* how they can ease your frustration. The problem is, we're often much better at talking about what we *don't* want rather than what we *do*. This makes coming up with three things that would feel good surprisingly difficult to do.

Many of us have been raised with messages like: "Do for others," "Don't think about yourself," and "Don't be selfish." As a result, it can be challenging to ask simply, clearly, and kindly for what we want and need. But if we don't learn how to do this, our needs won't get met.

So be creative. Ask for things that would be fun for you to receive and also fun for your partner to give. For the example we've used in this chapter, the three SMART requests might be:

1. We could alternate the holidays next year, spending one with your family and the next one with mine.
2. We could set aside a special time in the next two months to invite my family to visit.
3. We could choose one holiday to host this year and call both our families this weekend to invite them to attend.

If you wanted to get even more creative, you could suggest something like: We could create a photo album together that shows my family how much they mean to us. Or (if family finances allow) we could book a cruise or rent a cabin by a lake and have a holiday with my family. Whenever possible, requests should be lighthearted, even whimsical. They should never feel like a punishment to your partner. Again, the important thing is to make requests that help set your partner up for success.

As the Sender shares each idea, the Receiver writes it down. They can even Mirror each idea back to be sure they got it right. And after the Sender shares all three ideas, the Receiver chooses one.

Now the two of you are on your way to a Partnership Marriage (where not only your holidays, but your relationship itself, feels more equal!). It is delightful to be connected with someone when there is mutual respect and problem solving instead of blaming and shaming.

It feels great to be connected!

START WITH THE MOLE HILL, NOT THE MOUNTAIN . . .

A word of caution: Start off small—with the mole hill rather than the mountain. We know you've probably got *a lot* of things you're frustrated about.

But go slow here. Remember, often what we want most from our partner are the things that are hardest for our partner to give. When your partner succeeds with the easy things, they can then grow to take on the bigger challenges.

For example, your frustration might be: "I feel like we don't spend time together anymore." Of the options you offer, your partner may choose to cuddle with you on the couch for at least fifteen minutes every evening for a week—and then *actually do it*. Meeting your request might feel good to your partner: Even though you're asking something of them, you're still giving them a choice. And it can be such a *relief* to them when they know exactly what to do!

Following through on what they said they would do empowers your partner. And what do you think they're going to want to do with that wonderful feeling of empowerment surging through their veins? You got it—take on some more! Set them up for success and they will be happy to do this again and again.

Criticism kills your partner's motivation. Many of us are so good at proving to our partners what failures they are, that they give up hope. Your job is to encourage and empower your partner, and the BCR can help them get there! Before you know it, you'll be resting in a Space Between that's glowing with love.

The BCR teaches both you and your partner to stretch.

Your partner will grow by agreeing to—and actually following through with—one of your three requests. And you will grow by receiving what they offer, which is a gift to them as well.

Truth #7: Negativity Is a Wish in Disguise

EXERCISE: THE BEHAVIOR CHANGE REQUEST (BCR)

First:

1. Choose a frustration you've experienced with your partner (if you can't think of any at the moment, refer back to the list you made during exercise #1, "Then and Now"). Start with the mole hill, NOT the mountain— you want to set both of you up for success.

2. Use the detailed steps that follow to walk yourselves through the BCR.

    And go to **www.MakingMarriageSimple.com** *for video examples and other resources.*

Step One: Ask for an Appointment

The Sender asks for an appointment:

> **Sender:** *I'd love to talk with you about a request I have. Would now be okay?*

Step Two: Briefly Describe Your Frustration

Using Sender Responsibility, the Sender briefly describes their frustration in one sentence (two at most). An example of a simply stated frustration might be (though you should obviously use your own):

> **Sender:** *I get frustrated when you come home later than you say you will.*

The Receiver then Mirrors back exactly what the Sender said:

Receiver: *So let me see if I got it.* [Repeat word for word the frustration your partner just shared with you. For the example above, this would be: "You get frustrated when I come home later than I say I will."] *Did I get it?*

Once the Sender confirms that the Receiver got it, the Receiver asks: "**Is there more?**" Remember, don't flood your partner. An example might be:

Sender: *When you're not on time, I worry about you.*

The Receiver then Mirrors this new statement, and once the Sender confirms that the Receiver got it, the Receiver Validates and Empathizes with the Sender:

Receiver: *It makes sense that you get frustrated and worry when I come home later than I say I will (Validate). And I can imagine that this makes you feel sad and angry (Empathize).*

Step Three: The SMART Request

Once the Receiver Mirrors, Validates, and Empathizes with the Sender, and the Sender feels understood and acknowledged, the Receiver asks for three requests. And the Sender answers clearly and specifically with three things that would help.

Receiver: *How can I help you with that? Give me three options.*

Sender: *Thank you for asking! Here are three things that could address the issue:*

1. You could give me one back rub (or something a bit steamier!) one night a week for the next month.
2. You could bring me breakfast in bed one Saturday or Sunday a month for the next two months.
3. You could do the grocery shopping once a week for a month.

> *Note: While four backrubs, two breakfasts in bed, or four trips to the grocery store might seem out of proportion to the frustration, we've got a reason. Our brain's default is to dwell on the negative. So it takes repetition of the positive to counteract that. It may not seem logical, but this is how our brains work. Combating the negative with a solid dose of the positive is one way to train your brain (more on this in Truth #8, Your Brain Has a Mind of Its Own).*

Then:

Continue to use the BCR, taking turns being the Sender and Receiver. Use smaller frustrations at first (remember, mole hill—not mountain!). As you both become comfortable with the process, you can bring the more challenging frustrations to each other. It's always good, however, to alternate nights instead of both having a turn one right after the other on the same night. In fact, unless you and your partner are doing the Exercise Program as a weekend or weeklong retreat (see page 150), we suggest having one partner be the Sender one week, and the other partner be the Sender the following week. Doing this allows each partner to truly experience that their mate has heard their frustration.

As the Receiver, it is a good idea to tape the request you've agreed to meet on the wall where you can see it every day. Then follow through on what you've agreed to. When the Receiver has followed through on the request, it's time for both of you to celebrate!

And Remember:
Taking small steps with the Behavior Change Request
empowers you both.
And what you'll want to do with that empowerment
is take on some more—until all the issues
in your relationship feel solved!

TRUTH #8

Your Brain Has a Mind of Its Own

HELEN

Our brain is a wonder. It is the seat of our emotions and thoughts. It determines why we feel the way we feel, and why we think the thoughts we think. Scientists have explored and obsessed over the mysteries and intricacies of this organ, writing countless pages about their discoveries.

So what does brain science have to do with a book on marriage, you ask?

A lot!

A REPTILE AND A BIRD?

The brain can be divided into two parts: the lower brain, which we call the Crocodile; and the higher brain, which we call the Owl. The lower brain is often referred to as the reptilian center of the brain. Like the **Crocodile, it is highly reactive. It responds spontaneously without stopping to analyze a situation.** When you accidentally touch a hot stove, you immediately pull your hand back. The movement happens without your even thinking about it. That's your lower brain saving you from getting burned.

This lower brain has a pretty straightforward job description:

SURVIVAL. **It exists to defend itself (you) against danger.** It reacts faster than the speed of thought.

The majority of the time, Crocodiles laze around in the water. Still and quiet, you could mistake them for a log. Out of the water, you'll find them snoozing contentedly on a muddy riverbank. In this state, they seem placid and harmless. Who could possibly be afraid of such a sluggish beast?

When a Crocodile is threatened, however, WATCH OUT!

From the tip of their long snout to their powerfully thrashing tale, crocodiles become pure muscular destruction. A pissed-off Crocodile is PURE DANGER. This is why it's best not to provoke your partner's Crocodile. Especially at night! Who, after all, would want to sleep next to something that bumpy, with all those razor sharp teeth?

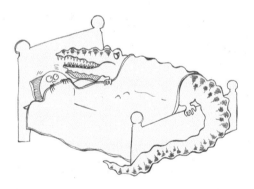

Fortunately, you also have your higher brain. We call it the Owl, and it can help you control your Crocodile. It wouldn't seem as though a feathered friend could make much headway against the Croc's muscular power. But the Owl's ability to observe and strategize can run circles around the Crocodile.

The Owl is the higher part of the Brain. It is capable of more creative and more sophisticated thinking. It catalogues your experiences, collects data, and problem-solves—constantly searching for more effective ways to do things. Because it connects higher brain intellect with memory and emotions, the Owl helps you manage your feelings.

Ultimately the Owl is great at creating win-win situations, so that everyone ends up safe and happy. In fact, it's the Owl that decided to buy this book!

Do you see these two different parts in yourself—the reactive Crocodile and the thoughtful and sensitive Owl?

Here's an example of the Crocodile surfacing in day-to-day life. Let's say you planned a fun little surprise for your partner. They were due home at six. . . .

It's now 6:30.

No partner. No phone call.

You keep checking your watch.

Now it's 7:15. . . .

What an *insult*! How **disrespectful**!

You get madder. . . . And MADDER . . .

By the time your partner walks through the door, the Crocodile is doing one of two things, depending on whether you're a Turtle or a Hailstorm.

The Turtle/Crocodile has completely withdrawn. Now, nothing short of a stick of dynamite is going to pry that Turtle out of its shell! All you're going to get if you're the late partner is an icy cold stare, as the Turtle/Croc's tail thrashes angrily from side to side.

The Hailstorm/Crocodile is lying in wait. Every ounce of their attention is focused on one thing: the clicking of the lock. And the minute they hear it, they SNAP! The late partner walks in the door expecting to find their mate. Instead, they get hit with the full force of a furious Croc—teeth bared, ready for battle! Nasty, isn't it?

When either of these scenarios happens, we say that the Crocodile has **hijacked your neural energy**. This means that your lower brain is so activated that you've temporarily lost access to your higher brain. Any chance of handling the situation gracefully is gone.

When we're in Crocodile mode, we have only two instinctual ways of responding: **with fight (the Hailstorm) or by taking flight (the Turtle).** No other options exist. Later, when our connection to the higher part of our brain is restored, we might say, "I'm sorry. I just lost my mind." And in a way we did. In that moment we lost contact with the higher, problem-solving part of our brain.

AND NOW FOR SOMETHING TRULY REMARKABLE . . .

You may think you've got no control over such an instinctual re-action. But you do! **You have the power to choose which part of your brain to use when interacting with and responding to your partner.** This does two very important things.

First, when you're upset about something your partner says or does, stopping to make a choice enables you to respond grace-fully instead of reacting in a way that creates or continues conflict. Second, the ability to choose helps you act and speak in ways that avoid pressing your partner's buttons in the first place. In other words, you can choose to act in ways that let your partner's sleeping Crocodile lie (how's that for mixing metaphors!).

So here we are, back at your house on that ill-fated night when you arranged that little surprise for your partner. And your partner was LATE.

Now what if, instead of giving in to the Crocodile, you reminded yourself to let the Owl review the situation? Believe it or not, **this one little decision has the power to stop the Crocodile *before* it starts to take control**. It seems too simple to be true—but it is. We're not saying that choosing to look at things from the Owl's perspective will wipe away all your frustration. But it will stop you from tumbling headfirst into the Crocodile's fight-or-flight response.

Now, instead of assuming you know why your partner is late, you can begin to wonder why (remember, get curious). You might even remember some details that could explain their tardiness. Notice that your anger and irritation fade the more you get curious.

You can even take some time to think about how the frustration you're feeling connects with any childhood experiences you remember. Were your parents often late? Did they ever disappoint you when you gave them a gift or did something special for them? Exploring possible connections between your current frustration and your past will help remind you that 90 percent of the issues we have with our partner are actually from our childhood.

If imagining different reasons why your partner might be late isn't taming the Crocodile as fast as you'd like, remind yourself that your partner obviously didn't know you were creating a surprise for them, so it's not like they *planned* to be late out of spite. You can also think about some of *your* less than perfect moments with your partner, and remember those times when your partner responded to your imperfections with care and understanding.

The goal at this point is to keep doing things that let the sleeping Crocodile lie. The Owl might suggest that you relax in front of the TV. Now would be a good time, after all, to watch that show you DVR'd last week—the one your partner wasn't interested in seeing. Or listen to some of your favorite music. You could even dust off the DVD of your wedding, or bring out your honeymoon photos.

If you still have some lingering frustration, a brisk walk around the block or some other form of exercise might help you calm down even more. Physical movement can really soothe the Crocodile.

So instead of getting hit with "WHERE THE HECK HAVE YOU BEEN YOU (enter choice phrase here)?!" your partner comes home to someone calm, collected, and concerned.

Rather than snapping, you can say something like "Wow, I expected you home at six tonight. I'd even planned a little surprise for us. I was getting a bit worried. Are you okay? What happened?" When your partner explains, say, "Let me see if I've got that," and Mirror them. Mirroring is like rubbing the Crocodile's belly, further calming the beast.

You don't need to have a formal Dialogue to use Mirroring. It's a great tool for calming yourself and your partner.

Once your mind is calm, it becomes possible for you to actually Validate and Empathize with your partner. You may discover that they lost track of time because of a work emergency, or there might have been an honest miscommunication between you. Once you realize that their actions and feelings are valid from *their* point of view, you're in the home stretch. Because this, more than anything else, shows you that you're experiencing your partner as a unique and separate person and not an extension of you.

Instead of being slammed over the head by a Crocodile's tail, your partner has been Mirrored, Validated, and Empathized with. Maybe you even share with your partner how this experience reminded you of your childhood—and they understand. Suddenly you're hearing your partner acknowledge how upsetting it must have been for *you* to go to all the trouble of setting up the surprise, only to have them not show up when you thought they were supposed to.

You partner apologizes.

You accept their apology.

And you hug and have a wonderful meal (reheated, of course).

Big sighs of relief all around!

Maybe you even co-create a plan where your partner takes initiative for the next romantic date time.

Congratulations! Here you've navigated Crocodile-infested waters, and both of your fearsome beasts have slept through the experience. Now you know that when your partner says or does something that activates your Crocodile, you can choose to *respond* in a way that builds connection instead of *reacting* in a way that destroys it.

Checking in with the Owl comes in handy when choosing how you talk to your partner as well. Before you bring up something that is a concern to you—or before you take an action that you know has triggered your partner in the past—ask yourself: **Will this thing I'm about to do or say set off my partner's Crocodile?**

Remember: You can't control your first thought. But you can, with the Owl's help, control the second!

The Crocodile isn't all bad. It's an important part of our brain, and we don't want to get rid of it. That would make us vulnerable in the face of real danger. We need it to access our instincts. We just want the Owl to help manage it.

Learning about the two parts of the brain was very empowering for me. I didn't want to be a grouchy Crocodile with Harville (not exactly the most loving choice!), nor did I want to be one with myself (all that dry skin!). So when I found out I had a choice, I did all I could to stay in the higher brain function of the Owl. It was amazing the impact that this alone had on our marriage.

Of course all this takes practice. But now you have a choice you didn't have before you read this book—and tools to help you. We can't control others (no matter how much we'd like to at times). The only thing we have control over is ourselves—our thoughts, responses, actions, and reactions. Understanding this keeps us focused on what we CAN change: ourselves. And stops us from focusing on what we can't change: our partner.

Learning how to choose between the Owl and Crocodile is a key part of taking this personal responsibility. Expect a transformation!

Truth #8: Your Brain Has a Mind of Its Own
EXERCISE: TRAIN YOUR BRAIN

First:

1. You will need 10 to 15 minutes for this exercise. Find a quiet place where you will not be disturbed. Sit in a comfortable chair, close your eyes, and for five minutes (you can use an egg timer or set the alarm on your phone) focus on your breathing and count your breaths. If you lose count, start over. Continue until the time is up.

2. Now bring to mind something about your partner that disturbs you. Hold it firmly in your mind for two deep breaths. Then let it go and immediately bring up something you love about your partner. Hold that firmly in your mind for five deep breaths. Repeat this for five minutes.

3. Now imagine your partner. Think about them on the day that you married. At a time when they were grieving. And/or at a time when you felt particularly proud of them. Holding this image in your mind, say out loud: "My partner is a human being. Like me, they try hard, make mistakes, feel pain, and want to be loved." From this place, send your partner loving thoughts.

Then:

Continue this exercise for the remainder of your exercise program, adding it to the days when you're already sharing

Appreciations with each other. The goal is to practice to the point where you are able to get to this meditative place easily. This will make staying connected with the Owl a breeze as you listen to your partner's frustrations.

And Remember:

You have the power to rewire your brain.
Building a Partnership Marriage actually changes your
brain chemistry, creating new neural pathways
to support the work you're doing.

TRUTH # 9

Your Marriage Is a Laughing Matter

HARVILLE

Let's face it, even the best relationships have deeply serious issues. Treating the issues seriously, however, is *not* the solution. Knowing when to be lighthearted is an art form. Also, many couples find themselves working so hard on their relationship, that they forget to actually have fun together.

A couple's wisdom about using humor and joy is critical to their happiness together. The sign of a relationship artist is someone who, even when they are dealing with hot-button issues, can touch on them lightly and bring in a spirit that allows for a mutually satisfactory solution.

After all, life isn't about our job, or who or what we know, or how much stuff we own. These things don't make us happy. It is about *who* we are at our core—and how healthy our connection is with each other.

At our core is JOY. It is our essential nature—with us from the moment of birth.

Birds have flocks. Dogs have packs. Horses have herds. And humans are wired for connection.

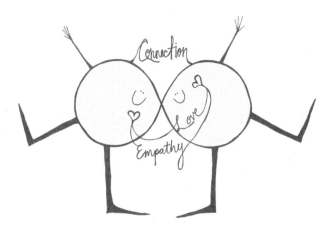

We are wired for connection!

Connection and joy are two sides of the same coin. You can't experience joy without being peacefully connected.

We believe that you were meant to live in this original, blissful, JOY!

Before you can ride off into the bliss, however, you have to wake up to a very important fact. There is one surefire way you can kill joy. . . .

RELATIONSHIP JEOPARDY IS NOT A GAME SHOW

Have you ever said to your partner (or secretly said to yourself) anything like the following:

"If my partner really loved me, they would know what I want . . ."

"We've been together for over twelve years. How can they not know . . ."

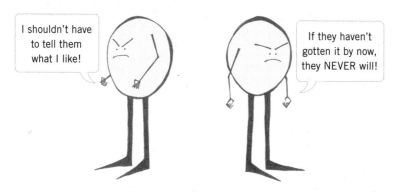

It doesn't matter if you've been together for two months or twenty-two years. If you have struggles in your relationship, it's likely because you:

1. **Expect your partner to know what you feel, want, and need** (without ever telling them); and/or

2. **Assume that you know how your partner feels and what they want** (without ever asking them).

Assuming your partner can read your mind or attempting to read theirs is as toxic as negativity. We call this "Relationship Jeopardy," and it's fatal to your marriage. Falling into either or both of these traps sucks the joy right out of your relationship.

When you expect, assume, and demand, you make your partner feel like an object. What you're ultimately communicating to your partner is: "You exist to meet MY needs." But if mind reading, expecting, and assuming are *not* the things to do—what should we do?

THE ULTIMATE CARE PACKAGE

ASK! Instead of assuming, you have to *ask* your partner what gives them pleasure. Then *really listen* to what your partner says, and give them what they ask for. And they need to do the same for you.

This leads us into the Caring Behaviors exercise. Caring Behaviors is *the* chance for you and your partner to share what specifically feels most caring to each of you. These are the behaviors you want from your partner, but have kept secret. The behaviors you hoped (okay, assumed) your partner would guess. The ones you blamed your partner for not doing. (And it's also nice to include the things your partner is *already doing* that feel caring to you.)

Whoa—here you've been blaming your partner for not figuring it all out. And all the while it was actually *your* responsibility to tell them. Everyone feels loved in different ways. Caring Behaviors can range from having your partner bring you a cup of coffee before you get out of bed in the morning, to having some uninterrupted time every other weekend so you can focus on home repair projects. One person may want a back rub, for another it's an occasional date night out on the town.

I was working with a couple who'd gotten stuck in the Caring Behaviors exercise. Now this hardly ever happens. Caring Behaviors is usually the time during our workshops when couples really relax and enjoy each other. So I asked them what was up.

"Well," she said, "I've always had this fantasy. . . ."

"But she won't tell me about it," her husband said.

"It has to do with when we're in bed," she confessed.

I encouraged her to tell him, but she was really struggling. Finally she motioned for me to bend down, and whispered what it was in my ear.

"There's nothing wrong with that," I affirmed. "I'm sure he'd love to hear it."

So she gulped, looked at her partner, and said, "I've always wanted you to suck my big toe when we were in bed."

The sweetest grin came across his face, and he said, "Sure!"

It's incredible to witness the deepening of connection between two people in love.

But this kind of magic won't happen if you keep silent.

You *have* to tell each other.

Take Helen and me, for instance. She used to think that since I loved *Star Trek*, I would like *Star Trek* paraphernalia. So she'd constantly surprise me with pens, mugs, bath towels, T-shirts. . . . If they made it with a *Star Trek* logo on it, you can rest assured that she added it to my collection.

Every time we shared Caring Behaviors it was on the tip of my tongue to tell her what I really wanted, but I didn't want to hurt her feelings. Finally, I knew I had to take the plunge. That night during our Caring Behaviors sharing, I said as gently as I could, "Helen, I appreciate your effort in buying me that *Star Trek* bath towel this week. But that isn't what makes me feel cared for. What has meaning for me is some uninterrupted time now and then to simply *watch* the show."

"OH!" she exclaimed, and laughed. "Gosh, Harville, you poor thing—you've got every *Star Trek* trinket known to human kind (and who knows what other aliens), and it's not even what you wanted."

I realized instantly that my worries about hurting her feelings were unnecessary. All Helen needed was the awareness of what I really wanted. Not only was she not upset, she was *delighted* with my honesty. And excited that, armed with this new information, she could hit a home run when it came to caring for me.

From that day forward, Helen stopped buying me *Star Trek* stuff. What she did instead touched me so deeply. When I'd set aside time for a *Star Trek* marathon, she'd slip into the room right before the show started. First she'd set down a tray of popcorn and homemade lemonade. Then she'd fluff up a comfy pillow and place it lovingly behind my head. With a sweet parting kiss, she'd leave me to it—and wouldn't interrupt me until I emerged from the room, done with my mini-marathon. It was absolute heaven!

So please, let your partner know your secret wishes!

Every couple of months you and your partner should spend thirty minutes writing down your Caring Behaviors, then post the lists where you will both see them every day. You can even use Dialogue to share them with each other. Some of the behaviors each of you asks for are going to feel easy to do. Some may not. Pick the ones that feel doable, and do them often. And watch your partner's pleasure blossom and grow!

The point is that **Caring Behaviors are a gift.**

But don't make the mistake of assuming this means that Caring Behaviors are all fluff. Engaging in them can slowly repair your partner's heart. Also, **requesting what you want shifts you out of the position of being a victim** faster than just about anything else in this book will. And you'll have FUN doing it!

Caring Behaviors also help train your brain. You know what it's like when you find the absolute perfect gift. You feel on top of the world, right? It's the same with Caring Behaviors. When you give one to your partner, you often end up feeling like it was *you* who received the gift. This is because the Crocodile doesn't know the difference between giving a gift to someone else and self-gifting.

Like air fresheners for your relationship, Caring Behaviors dispense the heady fragrance of lightness and joy.

And if you want to up the stakes, there are always Random

Droppings. (Don't worry! They're a lot nicer than they sound.) Random Droppings are those wistful wishes your partner mentions offhandedly but never expects to receive. It could be having the oil changed in the car, getting involved in a new hobby, or having a day off from the kids. Listen to your partner's Random Droppings, then pick one to surprise them with every month or so.

For example, Helen works really hard, and sometimes gets so involved in her work that she forgets about taking care of herself. One day as we walked to the office together, Helen wistfully mentioned how long it had been since she'd had time to do some yoga. Her schedule was really booked, but when I looked at her calendar, I noticed an hour and a half window that next week. So I found a teacher who would come to the house, and scheduled a surprise hour session for that time slot. Helen was simply delighted.

Picking up on a Random Dropping delivers a powerful message. It shows your partner: "**I pay attention to you. I listen when you dream out loud. You really matter to me—every moment of every day.**"

A LAUGH A DAY KEEPS THE DIVORCE LAWYER AWAY

There is a lot of science to back up the importance of having fun.

Joy activates your brain to produce and release more of the neurochemicals that make you feel happy and connected. In other words, joy makes your brain create more joy. Oxytocin, appropriately called the "love hormone," is one of these neurochemicals. Also called the "bonding hormone," oxytocin is responsible for the mother-child bond.

But men create oxytocin too. And far from being just a cuddly little love hormone, oxytocin has been proven to reduce stress, increase immunity, and lower blood pressure and the risk of heart disease.[1]

How amazing to realize that simply having fun with our partner offers such concrete and far-ranging effects. And perhaps one of the most stunning things of all is that—like opting for staying connected to the Owl instead of descending into the hostile turf of the Crocodile (see Truth #8, Your Brain Has a Mind of Its Own)—we have the power to choose this behavior. What an empowering way to live!

We can choose this path of empowerment simply by sharing Caring Behaviors, inviting laughter into our relationship, cuddling, and getting our bedroom groove on.

Who knew fun had such power?

Now, when we tell you to bring laughter into your relationship, we know it may not be as easy for you as we might be making it sound. It certainly wasn't for us, at least. Helen and I are nerdy types. We're fun-impaired and humor-deficient. If that sentence is funny, it's only because we worked hard on it (and if you didn't find it funny, be gentle with us, we're still working on our sense of humor).

We realized we needed to bring more fun and lightness into our lives together. So we started by memorizing and telling each other jokes, watching the *Late Show with David Letterman*, and renting funny movies to watch together. One night we made dinner wearing Groucho Marx glasses and kept them on through the entire meal. Silliness doesn't come easily to us. That was a breakthrough dinner!

Another way we brought humor into our relationship was with "jump-start belly laughing." In this exercise you face each other, open your mouth, and say "hah, hah, hah" while jumping up and down. We know that you might be rolling your eyes right now. Yes, this is a silly exercise—*that's the whole point.*

It's impossible to laugh and be defended at the same time.

In fact, the Turtle, Hailstorm, and Crocodile don't have a funny bone among them.

Not a funny bone in sight.

Like Dialogue (Truth #5, It's Not WHAT You Say; It's HOW You Say It), stretching into some of these fun-fueling behaviors can feel uncomfortable. *Of course* Helen and I felt silly in the Groucho glasses (which, again, was the point). And we didn't dare use them when our children were in town—they already think we're pretty strange.

The thing to remember is that this kind of discomfort is good. It means you're growing. Don't forget the Stretching Principle (Truth #3, Conflict Is Growth Trying to Happen). It is the behaviors that push you out of your comfort zone that lead to joy. **A great relationship awaits you just beyond the borders of your comfort zone.** So if you wind up feeling foolish or uncertain, you can take heart in the knowledge that you're growing into new behaviors and getting your joy groove back!

Truth #9: Your Marriage Is a Laughing Matter
EXERCISE: DIALING IN JOY!

First:

1. Write down all the behaviors that feel most caring to you (see "Caring Behaviors" on page 186). These are the secret wishes that you expected your partner to figure out without your having to tell them. This list can also include things your partner already does (reinforce the good stuff, and they'll keep on doing it!).

2. Post the lists where you'll see them every day (next to the bathroom mirror, for instance, or on the refrigerator).

   And go to **www.MakingMarriageSimple.com** *for video examples and other resources.*

Then:

Some of the behaviors each of you asks for are going to feel spot-on for the other to do. Some may not. Pick the ones that feel doable, or even excite you when you think about doing them—*and do them*. Every couple of months you and your partner should spend thirty minutes adding to your written list. You can even practice Dialogue by sharing them.

And Remember:

Your partner is longing to be a hero or she-ro to you.
Often all it takes is the awareness ("Oh, this is what feels caring to you!") to make the shift.

Your Marriage Is the Best Life Insurance Plan

HARVILLE

I love *Star Trek* (as you know by now!). Just as you've learned not to flood your partner with rambling words, Helen has taught me not to flood others with *Star Trek* references. Yet it was *Star Trek* that long ago planted a seed—one that grew into a lifelong vision. And this vision happens to be the central theme of this chapter.

The Vulcan, Mr. Spock, is a favorite character of mine. The Turtle in me appreciates his rationality and ability to stay calm under the most challenging circumstances.

Turtles may seem oblivious at times (okay, a *lot* of the time). But they actually carry great depth and caring. And I'm not just saying this because I'm a Turtle!

More even than his rational mind, though, it was Spock's good-bye blessing that inspired me: "Live long and prosper, and let peace be in your land." From the beginning of our work together, this blessing summed up *why* Helen and I do what we do. Helen agrees (proving she truly *did* "get curious" about my interests).

What Helen and I want most in the world is to help couples "live long and prosper." We want this for *your* happiness and fulfillment. And also because we know it is *the* best way to "let peace be in our land" (but more on that in the Afterword).

From the start, Helen and I believed that a healthy marriage has far-ranging benefits, not just for individuals, but for society. But we didn't have the facts to prove it. So we began collecting statistics. And we're constantly finding new studies that confirm what we've intuited for years.

MAKING THE CASE FOR MARRIAGE

In the introduction we talked about the old model of marriage in which one person led and the other followed—in many cultures, ours included, the husband was in charge of the family, and the wife's thoughts and needs came second. For a long time this arrangement seemed to work just fine. Then in the 1960s and 1970s, women began questioning whether this model of marriage was really useful for them.

A new form of marriage, the Partnership Marriage, was struggling to be born.

But people didn't have the skills to nurture this new model. And divorce, once considered taboo, began slowly gaining in acceptance.

In time, therapists, theorists, and various doctors began

to assert that divorce was the best option for many couples in conflict—and even for their children. Indeed, Helen and I are both divorced. The thing is: If we'd had the tools in our first marriages that we have now, neither of our divorces would have happened.

Because so many couples still *don't* have the skills to heal their marriages, half of the married population continues to divorce. But this opt-out clause is not without consequences. Almost half of American families experience poverty following a divorce.[1] And when parents get divorced, it almost *doubles* the odds that their children will end up divorced as well.[2] This cycle is one we now believe is damaging for all involved.

But there is also good news. We're becoming aware of the benefits of marriage. Over the last fifty years, scientists have been documenting what has come to be called the **"marriage advantage."** Why is it called this? Because **married people, on average, are healthier, live longer, enjoy higher incomes, and raise healthier families.** And this is true for most marriages, whether they are "happy" or not.

The thing is: If just *being* married offers great benefits, imagine what a *healthy marriage* can accomplish. It will amplify your marriage advantage, all while creating the partnership of your dreams. What a great incentive for honing the skills to help make your marriage soar.

And now for the way marriage impacts the most important aspects of your life (drumroll please) . . .

FEELING BETTER, LIVING LONGER

Let's start with your physical health. **Married people are less likely to get pneumonia, have surgery, develop cancer, or have heart attacks.**[3] How incredible that simply saying "I do" has the power to lower your medical bills and protect your health.

Yeah, only regular checkups since I said "I do!"

If these findings weren't remarkable enough, now imagine what a healthy marriage could do. Studies show that our brains are structured to learn and thrive best when interacting with other brains.[4] In other words, we are meant to live in relation to others. And when our primary partnership is a healthy one, the intimacy generated releases an abundance of oxytocin. As you'll remember, this juicy "love hormone" has been proven to have a whole bunch of health benefits. You'll be bolstered not only by virtue of your partnership, but by the emotional and spiritual wholeness you're creating together.

CHILDREN WHO THRIVE

Those of you with children know that, as parents, we worry about *everything*. Are our kids eating right? Building strong friendships? Doing well in school? We're concerned because we want our children to become happy and self-reliant adults.

Well, guess what? Children whose parents are married tend to be more academically successful, more emotionally stable, and more often assume leadership roles.[5] Children with married parents also do less drugs and commit fewer crimes.[6]

And saying "I do" helps make all of this happen.

Now imagine the benefits your children could receive from a *healthy* marriage. One in which you and your partner model genuine respect, while sharing in the many responsibilities necessary to build a fulfilling life. Children raised this way will grow up knowing how to "live long and prosper and let peace be in our land."

What a great two-for-one. **Create a Partnership Marriage and our kids grow healthy and strong in the process.** It turns out the most important thing you can do for your kids is focus on creating Real Love. Your kids will soak it up. So feel free to toss out those stacks of parenting books.

GREATER FINANCIAL SECURITY

Now, let's explore the subject of money. Those who have gone through a divorce know how hard it can be financially. It's simple mathematics. Two people who once supported one household now have to support two. Everyone's lifestyle takes a dip.

Aside from avoiding the costs of divorce, however, married couples create more wealth.[7] Married households have, on average, about double the income and four times the net worth of the divorced or never married.[8]

Double the household income could easily be the difference between living on (or even under) one's income, versus running up credit card debt. Extra income could also enable a family to take trips, have money to repair the car (or even buy a newer one), help the children to graduate from college with less, or even no, debt, or bolster savings and retirement accounts.

This means greater security and more options for your family.

And although healthy marriages don't automatically create larger paychecks, they do produce couples who can better navigate win-win solutions. Less arguing about money means you'll spend more time enjoying each other. Aside from one of the more obvious ways couples enjoy each other, you can also practice the Dialogue exercise to share Appreciations (Truth #5, It's Not WHAT You Say; It's HOW You Say It). And you can use the resulting mellow mood to share some behaviors that feel particularly caring for you (Truth #9, Your Marriage Is a Laughing Matter).

Now this is the kind of cycle we like to encourage!

BEDROOM BENEFITS

This next finding is a really big surprise. It turns out that **married people have more sex *and* a better quality of sex** than single, divorced, or cohabiting individuals.[9]

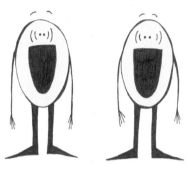

"WOW! Who knew?!"

How's that for a long-standing myth debunked? Most people assume that sex becomes virtually nonexistent when you're married.

Obviously there are times when couples fail to experience a meeting of the minds (or bodies). During these dry spells the grass can definitely look greener anywhere other than *in* the marriage.

So if you feel like everyone is getting some but you, take heart! Channel your passion into creating a healthy marriage. It will help both you and your partner manifest *all* your dreams (including those in the bedroom). As Real Love builds between two people, so does intimacy. Psychologists say that the most important sex organ is the brain. So focus on training your brain. It will release that "love hormone" oxytocin, which absolutely leads to amorous thoughts, feelings, and deeds.

It's amazing to realize that these marriage advantage benefits apply to most run-of-the-mill marriages. But Helen and I think this is because it is hard to quantify the impacts of "happy" marriages. We do know that stressful marriages have been shown to lower immunity and increase depression. In fact, a recent study suggests that a stressful marriage can be as bad on the heart as a regular smoking habit.[10]

Wow! What this tells Helen and me is that it's probably the stronger marriages that offer these tremendous advantages in your life—and **by building** *healthy,* **strong marriages, the impacts would be off the charts**!

So why not go for the gold?

With this book in your hands it has never been simpler to create the marriage of your dreams. To do this requires daily work, of course. It won't always be easy. But isn't a little effort, and having to sacrifice being "right," worth the rewards?

YOUR RELATIONSHIP IS WORTH IT!

I want to share another story. Not about Helen and me, this time—but about a couple in one of our workshops. They showed up deadlocked in the Power Struggle. In fact, they'd already filed for divorce.

She was ready to *explode.* He sat, passive in the face of her rage.

"Ah-ha," we thought, "the Hailstorm has met the Turtle. They are perfectly matched!"

But would they experience a breakthrough? Their early Dialogue exercises did not go well. Fists clenched, she'd practically be yelling. Silently seething with rage, he'd retreat even more deeply into his shell. For most of the first day we wondered if they'd even stay for the whole weekend.

But on day two they began making real progress in their Dialogue sessions. Soon, they felt safe enough to drop their defenses. Awestruck, we watched as their anger melted away, revealing the love and compassion they'd had for each other all along.

As couples shared comments about their experiences at the end of our time together, this couple stood. Holding up their divorce papers, the husband ceremoniously tore them up. Then, with moist eyes and a gruff voice, he announced: **"I came here with my biggest enemy and am leaving with my best friend."**

This is an example of the transformation we see, couple after couple, in those who commit to the ideas we've shared.

And we feel honored to bear witness to it each and every time.

So don't stay on the sidelines, reading this book while continuing to wish your partner were different. **Be the change you wish to see. Start modeling for your partner the spirit of kindness you long for *them* to bring to *you*.**

Start it, and your partner will join you in time.

Safety is contagious. Laughter is contagious. Lightness is contagious.

Love is contagious.

Love is contagious!

The more you practice, the stronger your relationship will become. Until you experience a profound communion no one can take away from you.

CELEBRATING YOUR RE-CONNECTION

Helen and I actually reached the Promised Land of this communion. Feeling joyfully alive, we had to stop ourselves from shouting our happiness from the top of the tallest building in New York (yes, even I, the Turtle, felt this way).

Instead of doing that, we created a re-commitment ceremony and decided to follow it up with a big party to celebrate. This is not normally our style. I'm more of a home cooking served on paper plates in the back yard kind of guy. But Partnership Marriage takes you into undiscovered territory.

By picking up this book, you've "boldly gone where a relative few couples have gone before." And we believe your willingness to do the hard work of stretching deserves a celebration. It is about re-committing to each other from this new awareness that you've created. Knowing that, **together, you have all that you need to "live long and prosper."**

Don't worry. You don't have to invite everyone you know to a gala event, march on Washington, or even leave home. It's just really nice, at this juncture, to renew your commitment to each other in whatever way suits you both best.

Truth #10: Your Marriage Is the Best Life Insurance Plan
EXERCISE: IT'S TIME TO RE-COMMIT

First:

1. Write down the vows you want to make to your partner today (see "My Vows to Our Relationship" on page 190). As you consider what you want to write, reflect on your journey of creating Real Love. Loosened from the force of Romantic Love and free from the Power Struggle, what can you vow to your partner now?

2. Once you both have finished your written statements, share your vows with each other. You can do this right after you've written them, sitting on your bed in your sweatpants. Or you can wait and share them during a re-commitment ceremony in front of family and friends (or both!).

3. Plan a way to celebrate your re-commitment to each other and the process of creating Real Love. There are so many ways you can do this:
   - Have an actual re-commitment ceremony.
   - Throw ceremony to the wind and just have a big party.
   - Go away for a romantic weekend or week—a second honeymoon. And share your vows with each other in the midst of an apple orchard or on a beach.
   - Do something completely out of the box, or even out of character, such as skydiving or hot air ballooning. Something that maybe you've both wanted

to do, but never made a priority. This could include renting Harley-Davidson motorcycles and attending a rally, taking a trip to an exotic location, hiking to the bottom of the Grand Canyon (and back out), or camping out for a week.

Then:

Put your vows into practice, using them as inspiration to continue to create the relationship of your dreams!

<u>*And Remember:*</u>

Be the change you wish to see!

The Relationship Revolution

HELEN AND HARVILLE

We wrote this book to share with you the culmination of our work so far. Our goal was to give you the most simple and effective ways to make your marriage great. We've offered you ten powerful truths to change your understanding about what makes relationship work (or not). Each one of these truths has been offered to shift your understanding about what is needed to create a successful partnership. And now, as we come to the end of our time with you, we want to give you the biggest shift of all.

You may think you purchased this book to breathe new life into your relationship.

This is true.

But that's not the whole story.

YOUR MARRIAGE, THE BETWEEN AND BEYOND . . .

In the last chapter, we shared some statistics with you about the impact marriage has on the two who say "I do." For those of you who are curious and want to know: "Is there more?" we have some important news to share about how marriage impacts our broader society.

Imagine the following newspaper headlines:

*Economists Predict an End to Global Poverty in the
    Next Five Years!*
CEOs Share the Wealth by Raising Employee Salaries
Heart Disease on the Decline
*More Prisons Closing as Nationwide Crime Drop
    Continues*

What could happen to cause these dramatic shifts? It could all start when people choose to shift from judgment to curiosity. Then, liking how this felt, they deliberately decide to give up negativity, growing empathic instead. Honoring each other's uniqueness, they speak more respectfully to one another. In other words, what makes this possible is when **couples begin to practice important new relationship skills in their marriages. Because doing this transforms how they feel about and interact with the world around them.**

LOVE: THE ULTIMATE UPSTREAM SOLUTION

In these pages, we've distilled the essence of the work you as a couple need to do, making it as simple as possible. But we don't make the mistake of assuming "simple" means "easy." We know this work is challenging. So, we want to remind you of the many reasons why it's worth doing.

Divorce is costly for the fractured family, as we confirmed in the last chapter. But this is just the beginning. Estimates on the average cost of a divorce in the United States range from $15,000 to $30,000.[1] Divorce and unwed childbearing cost American taxpayers an estimated $112 billion each year, and at least $1 trillion over a decade.[2] And it is our taxes that fund the agencies bearing the burden of these costs.

According to a special report: "even very small increases in stable marriage rates would result in very large returns to taxpayers. For example, a mere 1 percent reduction in rates of family fragmentation would save taxpayers $1.12 billion annually."[3] One percent! And our government could have an extra billion plus a year to spend on other things.

How's that for lowering the deficit. And not by cutting any programs—but by enhancing the quality of relationships!

Marriage didn't always hold this kind of potential. Feminist icon Gloria Steinem spoke for many women when she said back in the '70s, that marriage is a dangerous place for women. This was due to the dominator/submissive model of traditional heterosexual marriages. Therefore, for women to become strong within themselves, some had to leave home—and still others had to leave their marriage.

The Partnership Marriage changes all this. Once two people learn to live in a conscious partnership, the process can help women develop their most resonant voice and deepest wisdom. Within a respectful relational paradigm, both women and men can now flourish.

So if we're looking for ways to help strengthen our society, there is a growing new consciousness that holds wisdom for us all. As we deliberately expand the marriage advantage into our culture, we offer five final truths to aid in this transformation (here you thought you were purchasing a book with ten truths, and we've given you an additional five for free!):

1. Healthy Marriages Are the Ultimate Upstream Prevention

Unfortunately, the headlines we read every day are very different from the ones listed earlier. Our society struggles with many issues, such as teen pregnancy, alcoholism, increased high-school dropout rates, and poverty—to name a few.

Focusing on these issues is what we call "downriver cleanup."

Of course you want to clean up a river that's full of pollution. But sooner or later it will get polluted again. Which means you'll have to clean it again. You'll have to *keep on cleaning up that same river over and over again.*

Our governments and so many private organizations pour billions of dollars into downriver cleanup. How about figuring out where the pollutants are coming from?

Downriver issues are symptomatic of an unhealthy community.

To go upstream, you've got to fix the community.

The core of any community is the family.

And the core of the family is the couple.

Put simply: **Healthy homes lead to a healthy society. And the way to ensure healthy homes is to have healthy couples.**

If you want to create a society full of individuals who know how to take personal responsibility, you have to create that at home. If you want to build more compassion and caring in the world, you have to build it at home. To build a healthy home, you have to heal the couple. Because couples are where our society comes from.

And it can be as simple as focusing on the ideas and exercises you learn in this book.

2. Healthy Relationships Create Strong Individuals

For years, it was believed that to become a strong individual you needed to focus on caring for yourself. The philosopher Socrates believed wisdom was born from "Knowing Thyself." "You Know the Self, By the Self" said Krishna, who is considered a Supreme Being and Deity in the Hindu tradition. "I Think Therefore I Am" declared another philosopher, Descartes. These are just three of the many who avow this approach.

We disagree. We believe that we discover who we are **in relationship, not in isolation. We are born in relationship. We are wounded in relationship. We are healed in relationship. We** cannot know or become who we are *except* in relationship. Essentially, we are our relationships. **And the most powerful relationship for self-discovery and transformation is our primary love relationship.** It is within this context that you can actually rewire your brain, shifting how you think and feel.

We are not alone in this belief. A subtle shift is rippling across the globe, one that moves us from a focus on the individual to a focus on the relationship. It is a paradigm shift from the self as center to the relationship as center. As the boundaries that separate states and even countries become more porous, we have come to realize that we not only *can't* escape each other—*we actually need each other*. More and more people are recognizing that we are wired for connection. That makes the key question: How can we be in healthy connection?

Committing to share a life with someone else is an honor and a responsibility. And we don't use those words lightly. The role of those choosing to commit to a life partner is that of friend, supporter, advocate, and healer. It is about growing oneself to take on the welfare of the other. **It is about committing to create a healthy relationship, in order to mature as an individual.**

3. Couplehood as a Spiritual Path

We once heard someone say: "If you want to test your level of enlightenment, spend a week with your family." Oh boy, can some of us relate!

Remind me again why it was a good idea
to come home for a visit. . . .

Many go on retreat by themselves to deepen their spiritual lives, which takes them out of their relationship. It's a great thing to do, and we have no quarrel with it. There's another way to evolve as a spiritual being. One that's closer to home, because you *actually stay at home.* It is by developing your capacity to authentically love an "other." Let's face it, feeling at peace is easy when removed from the everyday burdens of life. That's why people go on vacation.

It is a lot harder to find our peaceful center when looking into the face of another—especially when that "other" may not be feeling at peace with *us.* And when our beloved is bugging us, forget it. Peace flies right out the window!

For this reason, we say that **one of the greatest spiritual paths is staying put in your relationship and learning how to** *really love your partner,* **warts and all.** When you can validate your partner's experience and express empathy—even when their experience makes absolutely no sense to you.

I love you, warts and all!

Elevating your relationship to this status transforms the Imago Process into a spiritual practice. Like meditation and prayer, Dialogue slows you down, quiets your mind, and invites you to put aside those same old thoughts you obsessively think about over and over again. Instead, you simply Mirror back your partner's words, and imagine how they are feeling, truly bearing witness to their experience. Then when you offer them a Caring Behavior and speak to them from the Owl instead of the Crocodile, you are unleashing the neurochemistry of Love. This feels great to you, and is great for your partner.

The Divine is waiting to show up in the Space Between.

The Sacred Space created feels hallowed to you both.

Walking the path of a conscious marriage may not be easy, but it is truly a way to experience Heaven on earth. And you can always call on your Faith to give you strength. Learning to truly love each other will feel so good to you both, and the resulting sense of wonder will spill over into every other area of your life.

4. Marriage Isn't a Disease to Be Treated—It's the Cure

Too often, when a marriage gets stressed and the couple seeks help, we diagnose and/or medicate it (or one of the individuals within it). Or worse, we prescribe separation, hoping that some time apart will enable the individuals to get their acts together.

Then there is the opt-out clause, divorce. Some people then get remarried, trading one partnership in for another—like exchanging an article of clothing at the store that didn't quite fit right.

Again, we see it so very differently. To be honest, **what relationship isn't challenged in certain ways or at various times? This doesn't mean the relationship—or the institution of marriage itself—is flawed.**

Healthy marriages are the ultimate upstream prevention that can eradicate so much of the downriver cleanup done each day. We believe our focus should be on the potential marriage has to cure the culture. Let's start caring for the well-being of our marriages. As a national and global culture we need to treasure the art of creating healthy marriages.

Let's prioritize it.

Let's fund it.

Let's nurture it.

5. Relationship Education Must Be Supported and Made Available to Everyone

Want to practice medicine or law? You've got years of schooling ahead of you, then you've got to pass your medical exams or the bar to get your license. Want to become an electrician or a plumber? There are courses to take and tests to pass before you are licensed. To sell real estate or trade stock, you have to study and get a broker's license. Want to drive a boat or big rig? Yep, you have to study and pass a test to get a license.

Heck, even if you want to drive a car, you've got to practice and pass a test before you get your license.

To obtain a marriage license, however, all you have to do is drop twenty bucks at the county courthouse.

This just isn't enough.

It takes knowledge and commitment to create a transformed relationship. You have to learn and practice the skills necessary for each person to grow into their potential as healers of their relationship.

In order for this to happen, the whole culture needs to be supportive. Schools, religious institutions, community centers, mental health agencies, government programs, even marriage/ event planners—all of them need to work together. Everyone who has access to couples needs to prioritize the distribution of information that will help each and every couple build a healthy marriage.

We could even start earlier. There are currently schools that have added to their health curriculums—as early as the elementary-school level—a crash course in caring for babies (some of you might remember having to partner with a classmate and carry around an egg or a sack of flour for a week). So **imagine the strides we'd make if future generations learned early on the importance of caring for their committed relationship— along with some of the skills necessary to actually do it.**

And we *especially* need support at the government level. Imagine the creation of a Department of Healthy Relationships!

Working to make your marriage as strong and healthy as you can is *the* single most important thing you can do. It impacts you, your partner, your family, *and* our world. If we became intentional about ensuring the health of marriages, we could make real strides toward not only reducing our deficit, but creating a civilization based on love.

CREATING A TIPPING POINT

We believe so strongly in this vision that we, along with other leading relationship experts, have started organizing to make it happen. Our goals are twofold:

- To launch a global movement to raise public consciousness about the essential connection between healthy relationships and a healthy society.
- To establish the support of healthy relationships as a primary social value.

And you can help!

There are couples everywhere on the vanguard. Imago Therapy, on which this book is based, has already—with no funding and no strategic plan—spread to over thirty countries. There are many counselors, therapists, and clergy who have adopted key pieces of our theory for use in their own practice with couples. Add to that the depth of wisdom and the reach of those we've brought together to launch a global movement, and it becomes clear that the time to focus on creating healthy marriages has come.

A Relationship Revolution is happening.

It is a zeitgeist.

What now seems cutting edge will, one day soon, be the prevailing wisdom.

And, of course, the most crucial component of this movement is each individual couple who courageously choose the path of creating the relationship of their dreams.

You, too, can join this Relationship Revolution. By purchasing and reading this book, you have unofficially become connected to this larger movement. Now we want to formally extend an invitation for you to join us. Add your voice to ours as we spread this message to every corner of the globe.

What can this look like?

First and foremost, it's about continuing to do what you're already doing—which is recognizing the importance of your relationship and caring for it and each other.

You can also share this book and those by our colleagues—or simply the ideas within them—with your family and friends, and even your work buddies.

If this idea leaves you feeling uneasy, remember those dark moments when your relationship was struggling. So many of the couples in our workshops have shared how alone they felt. From the outside looking in everyone else seemed to have the perfect relationship. Believing this, the misery these couples felt wound up being compounded by shame.

For this Relationship Revolution to happen **we need to break** through this isolation. **We have to have honest conversations, be real about how hard marriage can get, and also believe in the breakthroughs that are possible.** It doesn't have to take much, nor do you have to share a lot of gory details. A simple "Wow, my partner and I were really in it the other day, and boy did we find something that helped," or "My partner and I felt so disconnected, and let me tell you how we got to a better place," or words to that effect, can work wonders. With this, you've planted a seed. And at some point, if another one of your friends is struggling, they will remember.

So add the building of healthy marriages into your next Thanksgiving Day blessing—and follow it up with some information while the turkey and stuffing are being passed around. Don't hesitate to share your experiences with a couple who you think might be struggling. Teach your kids to Dialogue. Gift this book to your children after they bring their first serious boyfriend or girlfriend home, or add it to a wedding shower gift.

Healthy marriages lead to healthy homes, which lead to a healthy society.

How refreshing. How true.

And (perhaps most appealing) how ultimately *achievable*.

We are devoted to building Partnership Marriages, one relationship at a time. It is why we wrote this book. Now it's up to you to chart the course of your marriage's future. Your commitment to this work connects you to our efforts and to thousands of other couples across the planet. Our numbers are growing daily.

We thank you for having the courage and sheer stubbornness to stick it out with us (and, more importantly, *with each other*!). As you continue on this journey, always remember: **You have the power to create the marriage of your dreams**. And when you do, you also contribute to creating a new world in which we all can live long and prosper.

With appreciation and blessings,

Harville and Helen

THE EXERCISE PROGRAM

HARVILLE AND HELEN

The following exercise program gives you the tools you need to create the relationship of your dreams. Following are the same exercises included at the end of each chapter, with space to do each one. You and your partner could also use a separate notebook or journal to record your thoughts and progress. Or you can each have your own copy of this book.

Our goal is to set you up for success!

WHERE THE MAGIC HAPPENS

The exercise program that follows contains all the exercises that came after each Truth. We recommend going through the exercises in the order they're presented the first time around, but that's not a hard-and-fast rule. Here are some ideas for creating your own program:

1. Create a set date night or date day once or twice a week (for example, Tuesday evening and/or Saturday afternoon). Choose a truth, commit to reading it beforehand, and doing the exercise connected with that truth during this scheduled time together. For example, if you choose to do the exercises once a week each Thursday, your exercise program would look like:

WEEK	SUNDAY	MONDAY	TUESDAY	WEDNESDAY	THURSDAY	FRIDAY	SATURDAY
1					*Truth #1: Then & Now*		
2					*Truth #2: Taming the Hailstorm & Coaxing the Turtle*		
3					*Truth #3: Misses & Wishes*		
4					*Truth #4: Spring Cleaning for the Between*		
5					*Truth #5: Imago Dialogue Process*		
6		*Practice Imago Dialogue Process*			*Truth #6: Ritual of Appreciations*	*Ritual of Appreciations*	*Ritual of Appreciations*
7	*Ritual of Appreciations*	*Ritual of Appreciations*	*Practice Imago Dialogue Process*	*Ritual of Appreciations*	*Truth #7: Behavior Change Request*	*Ritual of Appreciations*	*Ritual of Appreciations*
8	*Ritual of Appreciations*	*Ritual of Appreciations*	*Ritual of Appreciations*	*Next partner does BCR if both didn't go yesterday*	*Truth #8: Train Your Brain*	*Train Your Brain & Ritual of Appreciations*	*Train Your Brain & Ritual of Appreciations*
9	*Train Your Brain & Ritual of Appreciations*	*Train Your Brain & Ritual of Appreciations*	*Train Your Brain & Ritual of Appreciations*	*Train Your Brain & Ritual of Appreciations*	*Truth #9: Dialing In Joy!*	*Train Your Brain & Ritual of Appreciations*	*Train Your Brain & Ritual of Appreciations*
10	*Train Your Brain & Ritual of Appreciations*	*Train Your Brain & Ritual of Appreciations*	*Train Your Brain & Ritual of Appreciations*	*Train Your Brain & Ritual of Appreciations*	*Truth #10: It's Time to Re-Commit*	*If you'd like to deepen the work, continue with Train Your Brain & Ritual of Appreciations—using Dialogue & the BCR as needed.*	

*Note: We recommend continuing to do the exercises Ritual of Appreciations and Train Your Brain throughout the remainder of the exercise program (and even the remainder of your marriage!).

2. Retreat time! Plan a trip to a fun location or take a vacation in your own home. Create a schedule in advance for working on the exercises together (making sure that each of you has time to read through the Truths beforehand). A sample retreat program might be:

	DAY 1	DAY 2	DAY 3	DAY 4	DAY 5	DAY 6	DAY 7
AM		*Truth #2: Taming the Hailstorm & Coaxing the Turtle*	*Truth #4: Spring Cleaning for the Between*	*Truth #6: Ritual of Appreciations*	*Truth #7: Behavior Change Request (if both partners didn't do it yesterday)*	*Truth #9: Dialing In Joy!*	*Truth #10: It's Time to Re-Commit*
PM	*Truth #1: Then & Now*	*Truth #3: Misses & Wishes*	*Truth #5: Imago Dialogue Process*	*Truth #7: Behavior Change Request*	*Truth #8: Train Your Brain & Ritual of Appreciations*		
RIGHT BEFORE BED				*Ritual of Appreciations*	*Train Your Brain & Ritual of Appreciations*	*Train Your Brain & Ritual of Appreciations*	

KNOWLEDGE IS NOT ENOUGH

The act of building a Partnership Marriage is deeply empowering. Ultimately, it all comes down to *you*. Through the building of a healthy relationship, **you and your partner have the power to create the marriage of your dreams**. Engaging in this work enables you to rewire your brain, so that you're primed to enJOY even more of the amazing stuff your marriage and your life have to offer.

As you continue this work, there will be days—and even weeks at a time—when you'll feel on top of the world, as if you've got this whole Partnership Marriage down pat. Then there will be those moments when all you want to do is throw in the towel. This is *absolutely normal*. Please, don't despair when frustrations surface. Instead, be gentle with yourself. You have been stretching into new territory, and your brain is pressing the Reset button, trying to make you go back to the old way of doing things. Take some time off, have fun with each other, then start up the program again.

Knowledge may be power. But it isn't enough. We learned the hard way that insight alone only goes so far. It was when we committed to practicing the tools *every day* that the real shifts began to happen. And it was the cumulative impact of these shifts that led to the deep connection we have today.

If you're like just about every other couple we know, you'll probably have different levels of commitment (and enthusiasm) about going through the exercises. Generally this means Turtles (who are less inclined to follow directions) may need to stretch a bit. And Hailstorms (who tend to get overzealous about diving in and getting things done) may need to contain themselves just a tad.

And yes, this was absolutely true for us.

Harville: When Helen first approached me about doing the exercises I withdrew into my shell. Sure they'd helped other couples. Of course I knew that; I had created the exercises and had been teaching them for years. Yet I still found myself resisting the idea of *actually sitting down and doing them* myself.

Helen: And I knew, once Harville reluctantly agreed, that I had to—at all cost—remain mellow. If my type-A Hailstorm showed up on the scene, the effort would be over before it had even begun.

So even we had to go slowly at first. But it didn't take long before our relationship started feeling really, really good. And the more we practiced, the more fun it became. Pretty soon we were both ferociously guarding our exercise time—so that we could continue to let the good times roll!

So we urge you to commit to absorbing the ideas in this book *and* practicing the concepts through the exercises. It is this combination that is truly life transforming.

Taking the kinds of actions we've set up for you in the exercises requires you to do things differently than you were before (and let's face it, if what you'd been doing had worked, you wouldn't have picked up this book). Be prepared to stretch yourself—but if the Crocodile's tail starts thrashing too much, the Turtle can't be pried out of its shell, or the Hailstorm begins to rumble, remember to take a break. **Call on your Owl.** Remember Truth #9, Your Marriage Is a Laughing Matter: Go for a walk, watch a movie, make a meal together, or slip into the bedroom. Once you've relaxed a bit together and maybe let loose some oxytocin, you'll be ready to dive back in.

You can also, at any time, refer to our website (www.Making MarriageSimple.com) for more information. We've packed it full of stories, other exercises, and resource sections. There is also a list of Imago Therapists worldwide, and our current workshop schedule.

Truth #1: Romantic Love Is a Trick

EXERCISE: THEN AND NOW

Romantic Love, conspiring with your unconscious, caused you to fall in love with someone whose behaviors will trigger your early childhood wounds. Now, as an adult—in a committed partnership and using the tools we've presented in this book—you have the opportunity to create a different, happier outcome.

The first step is seeing the similarity between your partner and your parents. You might not get this right away. Remember, it isn't that your partner will look or necessarily even act like your parents. It's that *you will feel the same way with your partner that you felt with your parents*. Exploring this connection between past and present helps replace blame with curiosity and understanding, and creates the foundation of your present work with each other.

First:

1. Write down the frustrations you remember that you had with your childhood caregivers and how you felt (you can use "Frustrations Then and Now" on page 157, which is part of this exercise program). The frustrations can be a specific event or a general experience.

    Reminder: Caregivers include whoever was responsible for your care when you were a child, for example, a parent, older sibling, relative, or babysitter.

2. List the ongoing frustrations you have with your partner

and how these make you feel. List as many as you can—including both petty annoyances and those things that really irritate you.

3. Look over the two lists, noting any similarities.

Then:

Talk over the similarities between the two lists with your partner. As you share, you'll notice the curiosity growing between you. It's hard to feel curious and frustrated at the same time. In the exercise for Truth #7 (Negativity Is a Wish in Disguise), you will practice how to turn the more challenging frustrations you have with your partner into specific requests for growth and healing.

And Remember:

*Ninety percent of our frustrations with our partner
come from experiences from our past.
That means only 10 percent of the frustrations
you currently have are about each other.*

FRUSTRATIONS THEN & NOW

My Name: _____

My Childhood Frustrations

Childhood Frustrations	Feeling(s)
Example (general): When my father criticizes me all the time.	*Not good enough.*
Example (specific): When my older brother forgot my birthday.	*Angry/unimportant.*

My Frustrations with My Partner

Partner Frustration	Feeling(s)
Example (general): When you complain that the house is messy and disorganized.	*Not good enough.*
Example (specific): When I made a special meal for us last Friday and you played computer games for two hours.	*Angry/unimportant.*

FRUSTRATIONS THEN & NOW

My Name: _____

My Childhood Frustrations

Childhood Frustrations	Feeling(s)
Example (general): When my father criticizes me all the time.	*Not good enough.*
Example (specific): When my older brother forgot my birthday.	*Angry/unimportant.*

My Frustrations with My Partner

Partner Frustration	Feeling(s)
Example (general): When you complain that the house is messy and disorganized.	*Not good enough.*
Example (specific): When I made a special meal for us last Friday and you played computer games for two hours	*Angry/unimportant.*

Truth #2: Incompatibility Is Grounds for Marriage

EXERCISE: TAMING THE HAILSTORM AND COAXING OUT THE TURTLE

Incompatibility, and the resulting tension of opposites, is vital to the work of healing and growth. And one of the ways you and your partner are opposite is in how you respond to conflict.

As you read through Truth #2, you probably figured out pretty easily who was the Turtle and who was the Hailstorm. If not, take some time to go back and read through the descriptions and talk about it now. If the answers still elude you, think about how you react when you're really frustrated—and you can always ask your partner!

Knowing which you are is all well and good, but what can you do about it? Following are ideas that we, and the couples in our workshop, have found very useful. These ideas are great when you're in the midst of a struggle. But you can also use them *before* any conflict arises to avoid having the Hailstorm hail or the Turtle hide.

Coaxing That Turtle Out

You're a Hailstorm and your Turtle is firmly stuck in their shell. Here are some ideas for luring them out:

1. Ask them what they need right now. *Don't get upset if they aren't sure. Just ask the question, and then focus on being someone your partner feels safe confiding in.*

Become more curious about why your Turtle has a hard shell (and a soft belly).

2. Don't do anything. *This is the simplest (and generally most effective) option. But it's also often the hardest for a Hailstorm. The thing is, if you give your Turtle a bit of space, they will peek out of their shell before you know it—and you won't feel like you're in it alone anymore.*

3. Write a short, kind note of sincere praise, and leave it somewhere for them to find (e.g. on their desk, nightstand, in their briefcase, taped to the bathroom mirror). *This reminds the Turtle that they are appreciated.*

Calming the Hailstorm Down

You're a Turtle, and your Hailstorm is at full fury, pounding you with their golf-ball-sized hail. Here are some ideas to soothe the storm cloud away:

1. Leave them a token of appreciation—a flower, a kind note, or a favorite snack. *This little gesture lets them know you care about them, and that you're not withdrawing.*

2. Ask: "What's going on?" Listen, and repeat back what your Hailstorm says.

3. If you really want to calm the Hailstorm, you can ask: "Is there something I can do for you?" *More than anything, this will let the Hailstorm know that you've got their back. And having a partner who has their back means everything to the Hailstorm. The thing is, you've got to follow up and actually DO whatever it is that they've said*

you could do for them. Otherwise you can expect the hail you're receiving to get even bigger!

<u>*And Remember:*</u>
Incompatibility is not only grounds for marriage. . . .
    It's the opportunity to create a great marriage!

Truth # 3: Conflict Is Growth Trying to Happen
EXERCISE: MISSES AND WISHES

The conflict you're experiencing is normal. You are not alone. Every couple on the planet struggles at times. Whew! What a relief.

Conflict has a message. Something new is trying to emerge in your relationship. The more you can identify what is trying to emerge in your relationship, the easier it will be to create. And this exercise is going to help you do just that.

First:

1. Write down the things you loved about your relationship when you first met, and miss now (see "Misses and Wishes!" on page 164).
2. Next write down something you've been longing to feel in your relationship—something you've possibly never felt before.

Then:

Take turns sharing items from each list. As you do, it's natural for memories to come up. Share those too. For example, if one of your wishes is that you'd love to travel more often, this might lead you to a memory of a wonderful trip you took together early in your relationship. Sharing that memory—and even cuddling while you do it—will get your brain to release the love hormone oxytocin, which is responsible for the wonderful feelings you had when you were in the Romantic Love phase of your relationship.

You can also make a list of things you want to create in your relationship and hang it on the fridge. Some of these may be relatively small (like being more affectionate with each other or having friends over more), and some might be larger (like going on a second honeymoon). Having your relationship wishes in plain sight will remind you to focus on creating them.

And Remember:

By stretching to give your partner what they need, you grow new skills.

MISSES AND WISHES!

My Name: _____

MISS

I Loved when We . . .

Example (general): . . . had candlelight dinners together.

Example (specific): . . . went on a spontaneous trip to Boston for the weekend.

WISH

I Wish We Could . . .

Example (general): . . . have more spontaneous sex.

Example (specific): . . . go to a Broadway play together.

MISSES AND WISHES!

My Name: _____

MISS

I Loved when We . . .

Example (general): . . . *had candlelight dinners together.*

Example (specific): . . . *went on a spontaneous trip to Boston for the weekend.*

WISH

I Wish We Could . . .

Example (general): . . . *have more spontaneous sex.*

Example (specific): . . . *go to a Broadway play together.*

Truth #4: Being Present for Each Other Heals the Past

EXERCISE: "SPRING CLEANING" FOR THE SPACE BETWEEN

Ah, the Space Between—the invisible space that determines the health of your relationship. You can fill the Between with tension and conflict or you can fill the Between with love and safety. Here's an exercise that will help you transform your Between into Sacred Space.

First:

1. In the pictures on page 168–169, write your name in one of the small circles and your partner's name in the other.

2. In the large circle at the top, list as many thoughts, feelings, and behaviors as you can that describe the positive things in your Between, the things that are WONDERFUL. These are the things that bring safety, connection, and/or passion into your relationship, like: respect, love, co-parenting, date nights.

3. In the circle at the bottom, list as many thoughts, feelings, and behaviors as you can that describe the negative things in your Between, the things that are CHALLENGING. These are the things that bring doubt, disconnection, and/or upset into your relationship, like: distrust, criticizing, lack of intimacy, no fun.

Then:

Share with your partner how *they* contribute to what is *wonderful* in your relationship. *(For example: "The best thing I see you bring to our space is . . .")* Follow that up with how *you* contribute to the challenges. *(For example: "I feel I contribute to our challenges when I . . .")* Finally, explore some ideas together on how you both can increase the wonderful and remove the challenges so that you create safety in the Between, transforming it into Sacred Space.

And Remember:

One of the most beautiful and profound things
about relationship is that we're called into the role
of being each other's healer.
This means NO shame, blame, or criticism in your Between!

THE SPACE BETWEEN

My Name: _____

WONDERFUL

CHALLENGING

THE SPACE BETWEEN

My Name: _____

WONDERFUL

CHALLENGING

Truth #5: It's Not WHAT You Say; It's HOW You Say It

EXERCISE: THE IMAGO DIALOGUE PROCESS

Dialogue is a structured way of talking that builds empathic connection between you and your partner. Now it's your turn to engage in this evolutionary way of relating. The more you practice Dialogue, the more natural it will feel. So don't be surprised if you find yourself Mirroring, Validating, and Empathizing with your partner throughout the day as you share challenges and triumphs with each other. And definitely feel free to use it during unscheduled times when frustrations or something to celebrate about your relationship surfaces.

First:

1. Choose who will be the Sender and who will be the Receiver.
2. Pick a topic. We suggest you start with something positive like sharing an Appreciation about your partner or sharing something about your day at work.
3. To begin, the Sender asks the Receiver for an appointment by saying: "Are you available for an Imago Dialogue?"

    And go to **www.MakingMarriageSimple.com** *for video examples and other resources.*

Step One: Mirroring

The Sender states their message, using Sender Responsibility.

The Receiver reflects back ONLY what the Sender says using the following language: "So let me see if I got it. You *[insert here exactly what your partner said]*. Did I get it?"

After the Sender confirms that the Receiver got it, the Receiver asks: "Is there more?"

The Receiver continues Mirroring until the Sender feels fully heard.

Step Two: Validating

The Receiver Validates the Sender's point of view by simply acknowledging: "You make sense." And remember, agreement is not the goal.

Step Three: Empathizing

As the Receiver, try to relate to the feelings underneath the issue the Sender shared. Remember, there are four core feelings: mad, sad, glad, and scared.

So to Empathize, the Receiver says something like: "Given that *[insert once again what your partner said regarding the issue]*, I can imagine you might be feeling *[use a word or two that might describe your partner's emotional state]*."

Then check in with: "Is that what you're feeling?"

If the Sender says: "No, I'm really feeling *X*," then the Receiver Mirrors what the Sender said.

Once the Sender responds positively that the Receiver

got how they feel, you can switch. The Sender becomes the Receiver and the Receiver becomes the Sender.

The key to Dialogue is practice, practice, practice!

Then:

Continue practicing Dialogue. We suggest you set aside time for full Dialogues, *and* you can also practice randomly throughout the day. It helps train the brain! For example:

- "If I heard you correctly, you said pass the salt. Did I get it?" (Mirroring)
- "Is there more about that?"
- "So you just said you would rather I not make a mess right after you've worked hard to clean the kitchen. That makes sense." (Validating)
- "Wow, your boss said that to you? I can imagine this made you feel really happy and proud. Did I get it?" (Empathizing)

Every interaction is an opportunity to bring Dialogue into your lives. Have fun with it!

And Remember:
In Dialogue, agreement is not the goal.
The goal is to take turns and really listen to each other.

Truth #6: Negativity Is Invisible Abuse

EXERCISE: RITUAL OF APPRECIATIONS

Negativity is toxic to your relationship. We define negativity as any words, tone of voice, facial expressions, or behaviors your partner says feel negative to them. No growth can happen in a relationship that is full of negativity. So if you want you and your partner to grow, you need to detox your relationship of all negativity.

There were two main things that helped us—and thousands of other couples—end all negativity. First, shift from judgment to curiosity. This can be as simple as looking at your partner as though you're only just meeting them (and to make it fun you can even plan on arriving at a bar separately and introduce yourselves as though you've never met before).

Second, share what you appreciate about each other. As you remember, when we first started to do this, it was much easier to complain about what we didn't like. So our Appreciations sputtered out. The Ritual of Appreciations was such a crucial component of our relationship shift, that we created this exercise to make it easier for you. With it you can identify what you truly cherish about your partner.

Now it's time for you to focus on the good so you can make your relationship great!

First:

List your partner's physical characteristics, personality traits, behaviors, and global affirmations (e.g., they are terrific, thoughtful, fantastic) that you appreciate, love, admire, and cherish. ("Appreciating You!" on page 176 offers a table and examples.)

Then:

End each day sharing three things you appreciate about each other before going to bed. And commit to doing this Ritual of Appreciations for the remainder of your exercise program—whether you're doing one of the sample programs we offer here, or a program that you put together yourself—on the days when you don't have other exercises to do.

Remember, *no repetitions allowed*. You can start with the Appreciations you wrote on your list. But also pay attention to your partner each day from the perspective of what you appreciate about them. The point of this exercise is to shift your focus from what you don't like, to what you do. As your focus shifts, you'll both start seeing more and more of the things you like—and each of you will be inspired to do more for your relationship.

Once you've completed your exercise program, you can even continue giving Appreciations. Why not? It feels great, doesn't it?

<u>*And Remember:*</u>

Energy follows attention.
The more you focus on the good,
the more good there will be to focus on.

APPRECIATING YOU!

My Name: _____

I Love Your/How You . . .

Physical Characteristics	Personality Traits	Behaviors	Global Affirmations
Blue eyes	Funny	Read to Amanda every night	You're terrific!
The freckles on your face	Compassionate	Make coffee for me every morning	I can't believe I'm lucky enough to be married to you!

APPRECIATING YOU!

My Name: _____

I Love Your/How You . . .

Physical Characteristics	Personality Traits	Behaviors	Global Affirmations
Blue eyes	*Funny*	*Read to Amanda every night*	*You're terrific!*
The freckles on your face	*Compassionate*	*Make coffee for me every morning*	*I can't believe I'm lucky enough to be married to you!*

Truth #7: Negativity Is a Wish in Disguise

EXERCISE: THE BEHAVIOR CHANGE REQUEST

The Behavior Change Request (BCR) is the key to transforming your frustrations with your partner into growth. Remember, frustrations are really hidden wishes. They are a mask hiding what you really want and are not getting from your partner.

This exercise teaches you how to share these frustrations/wishes with your partner in ways that will be easier for them to hear. The BCR also gives you a format to use to make requests of your partner. It is through the meeting and receiving of these requests that you and your partner grow.

First:

1. Choose a frustration you've experienced with your partner (if you can't think of any at the moment, refer back to the list you made during exercise #1, "Then and Now"). Start with the mole hill, NOT the mountain—you want to set both of you up for success.

2. Use the detailed steps that follow to walk yourselves through the BCR.

   And go to **www.MakingMarriageSimple.com** *for video examples and other resources.*

Step One: Ask for an Appointment

The Sender asks for an appointment:

Sender: *I'd love to talk with you about a request I have. Would now be okay?*

Step Two: Briefly Describe Your Frustration

Using Sender Responsibility, the Sender briefly describes their frustration in one sentence (two at most). An example of a simply stated frustration might be (though you should obviously use your own):

Sender: *I get frustrated when you come home later than you say you will.*

The Receiver then Mirrors back exactly what the Sender said:

Receiver: *So let me see if I got it.* [Repeat word for word the frustration your partner just shared with you. For the example above, this would be: "You get frustrated when I come home later than I say I will."] *Did I get it?*

Once the Sender confirms that the Receiver got it, the Receiver asks: "**Is there more**?" Remember, don't flood your partner. An example might be:

Sender: *When you're not on time, I worry about you.*

The Receiver then Mirrors this new statement, and once the Sender confirms that the Receiver got it, the Receiver Validates and Empathizes with the Sender:

Receiver: *It makes sense that you get frustrated and worry when I come home later than I say I will (Validate). And I can imagine that this makes you feel sad and angry (Empathize).*

Step Three: The SMART Request

Once the Receiver Mirrors, Validates, and Empathizes with the Sender, and the Sender feels understood and acknowledged, the Receiver asks for three requests. And the Sender answers clearly and specifically with three things that would help:

> **Receiver:** *How can I help you with that? Give me three options.*
>
> **Sender:** *Thank you for asking! Here are three things that could address the issue:*

1. You could give me one back rub (or something a bit steamier!) one night a week for the next month.
2. You could bring me breakfast in bed one Saturday or Sunday a month for the next two months.
3. You could do the grocery shopping once a week for a month.

> *Note: While four backrubs, two breakfasts in bed, or four trips to the grocery store might seem out of proportion to the frustration, we've got a reason. Our brain's default is to dwell on the negative. So it takes repetition of the positive to counteract that. It may not seem logical, but this is how our brains work. Combating the negative with a solid dose of the positive is one way to train your brain (more on this in Truth #8, Your Brain Has a Mind of Its Own).*

Then:

Continue to use the BCR, taking turns being the Sender and Receiver. Use smaller frustrations at first (remember, mole hill—not mountain!). As you both become comfortable with the process, you can bring the more challenging frustrations to each other. It's always good, however, to alternate nights instead of both having a turn one right after the other on the same night. In fact, unless you and your partner are doing the Exercise Program as a weekend or weeklong retreat (see page 150), we suggest having one partner be the Sender one week, and the other partner be the Sender the following week. Doing this allows each partner to truly experience that their mate has heard their frustration.

As the Receiver, it is a good idea to tape the request you've agreed to meet on the wall where you can see it every day. Then follow through on what you've agreed to. When the Receiver has followed through on the request, it's time for both of you to celebrate!

And Remember:

Taking small steps with the Behavior Change Request empowers you both.
And what you'll want to do with that empowerment is take on some more—until all the issues in your relationship feel solved!

Truth #8: Your Brain Has a Mind of Its Own
EXERCISE: TRAIN YOUR BRAIN

Those who study the brain have shown that it is possible to train your neural pathways to create newer, healthier connections. For our purposes, we broke the very complex brain down into two sections: the lower, reactive part of the brain, the Crocodile. And the higher, responsive part of the brain that can create win-wins, the Owl.

This exercise will help you strengthen the higher part of your brain, so that it's easier to align yourself with the Owl. Sleep tight, Crocodile!

First:

1. You will need 10 to 15 minutes for this exercise. Find a quiet place where you will not be disturbed. Sit in a comfortable chair, close your eyes, and for five minutes (you can use an egg timer or set the alarm on your phone) focus on your breathing and count your breaths. If you lose count, start over. Continue until the time is up.

2. Now bring to mind something about your partner that disturbs you. Hold it firmly in your mind for two deep breaths. Then let it go and immediately bring up something you love about your partner. Hold that firmly in your mind for five deep breaths. Repeat this for five minutes.

3. Now imagine your partner. Think about them on the

day that you married. At a time when they were grieving. And/or at a time when you felt particularly proud
of them. Holding this image in your mind, say out loud:
"My partner is a human being. Like me, they try hard,
make mistakes, feel pain, and want to be loved." From
this place, send your partner loving thoughts.

Then:

Continue this exercise for the remainder of your exercise
program, adding it to the days when you're already sharing
Appreciations with each other. The goal is to practice to the
point where you are able to get to this meditative place easily. This will make staying connected with the Owl a breeze
as you listen to your partner's frustrations.

And Remember:

You have the power to rewire your brain.
Building a Partnership Marriage actually changes your
brain chemistry, creating new neural pathways
to support the work you're doing.

Truth #9: Your Marriage Is a Laughing Matter
EXERCISE: DIALING IN JOY!

Our core is joy. It is our essential nature. We experience
this joy when we are peacefully connected to our partner.
Seriousness kills joy. One way seriousness sneaks into a relationship is through Relationship Jeopardy. This includes:
assuming our partner knows what we want without telling
them. Expecting and demanding that our partner meet our
needs without telling them what our needs are; or assuming
we know what our partner wants without ever asking them.

In Truth #9 we offered you different ways to lighten up
your relationship. But the best way to stop the game of Relationship Jeopardy is through the sharing of Caring Behaviors. Here's how.

First:

1. Write down all the behaviors that feel most caring to
   you (see "Caring Behaviors" on page 186). These are
   the secret wishes that you expected your partner to figure out without your having to tell them. This list can
   also include things your partner already does (reinforce
   the good stuff, and they'll keep on doing it!).
2. Post the lists where you'll see them every day (next to
   the bathroom mirror, for instance, or on the refrigerator).

> *And go to* **www.MakingMarriageSimple.com** *for
> video examples and other resources.*

Then:

Some of the behaviors each of you asks for are going to feel spot-on for the other to do. Some may not. Pick the ones that feel doable, or even excite you when you think about doing them—*and do them*. Every couple of months you and your partner should spend thirty minutes adding to your written list. You can even practice Dialogue by sharing them.

And Remember:

Your partner is longing to be a hero or she-ro to you.
Often all it takes is the awareness ("Oh, this is what feels caring to you!") to make the shift.

CARING BEHAVIORS

My Name: _____

I feel/felt loved and cared about when you . . .

_____

_____

_____

_____

_____

_____

_____

_____

_____

_____

_____

_____

_____

_____

_____

_____

_____

_____

CARING BEHAVIORS

My Name: _____

I feel/felt loved and cared about when you . . .

_____

_____

_____

_____

_____

_____

_____

_____

_____

_____

_____

_____

_____

_____

_____

_____

_____

_____

_____

Truth #10: Marriage Is the Best Life Insurance Plan
EXERCISE: IT'S TIME TO RE-COMMIT

Now it's time to celebrate the wonderful, juicy stuff you've committed to creating in your relationship. And, given all you learned about the "marriage advantage" in Truth #10, if you're not married yet, maybe it's time to take the plunge!

Your re-commitment can include a big party like ours. Or it may simply be the two of you in a special place re-exchanging vows or creating new ones. You can do this where you first met or first took a trip together, or at a place where you've always wanted to visit. It can even be in the sanctity of your very own home.

The point is to stop and officially recognize the journey you've been on and will continue to travel together. It's about re-committing to each other from the new awareness you've cultivated through this shared work.

First:

1. Write down the vows you want to make to your partner today (see "My Vows to Our Relationship" on page 190). As you consider what you want to write, reflect on your journey of creating Real Love. Loosened from the force of Romantic Love and free from the Power Struggle, what can you vow to your partner now?

2. Once you both have finished your written statements, share your vows with each other. You can do this right after you've written them, sitting on your bed in your

sweatpants. Or you can wait and share them during a re-commitment ceremony in front of family and friends (or both!).

3. Plan a way to celebrate your re-commitment to each other and the process of creating Real Love. There are so many ways you can do this:

    •   Have an actual re-commitment ceremony.

    •   Throw ceremony to the wind and just have a big party.

    •   Go away for a romantic weekend or week—a second honeymoon. And share your vows with each other in the midst of an apple orchard or on a beach.

    •   Do something completely out of the box, or even out of character, such as skydiving or hot air ballooning. Something that maybe you've both wanted to do, but never made a priority. This could include renting Harley-Davidson motorcycles and attending a rally, taking a trip to an exotic location, hiking to the bottom of the Grand Canyon (and back out), or camping out for a week.

Then:

Put your vows into practice, using them as inspiration to continue to create the relationship of your dreams!

And Remember:

Be the change you wish to see!

MY VOWS TO OUR RELATIONSHIP

My Name: _____

Today's Date: _____ My Vows to: _____

_____

_____

_____

_____

_____

_____

_____

_____

_____

_____

_____

_____

_____

_____

_____

_____

_____

_____

_____

MY VOWS TO OUR RELATIONSHIP

My Name: _____

Today's Date: _____ My Vows to: _____

_____

_____

_____

_____

_____

_____

_____

_____

_____

_____

_____

_____

_____

_____

_____

_____

_____

_____

_____

_____

_____

Notes

Truth #9: Your Marriage Is a Laughing Matter

1. Elizabeth Kowal, "Oxytocin, the Love Hormone, Has Health Benefits for Both Genders," *Health & Fitness,* October 24, 2009; http://www.examiner.com/article/oxytocin-the-love-hormone-has-health-benefits-for-both-genders (4/30/2012).

Truth #10: Your Marriage Is the Best Life Insurance Plan

1. California Healthy Marriages Coalition, "Healthy Marriages, Healthy Society: Research on the Alignment of Marital Outcomes, Marriage Education, and the Key Social Concerns," 2009; http://www/camarriage.com/content/resources/1f250f81-d24d-4937-9ce1-595464e2b6c8.pdf (9/17/12), p. 17.

2. Institute for American Values, "Why Marriage Matters, Third Edition, Thirty Conclusions from the Social Sciences," a report from a team of family scholars chaired by W. Bradford Wilcox of the University of Virginia, 2001, p. 19.

3. Tara Parker-Pope, "Is Marriage Good for Your Health?" *New York Times Magazine,* April 12, 2010; http://www.nytimes.com/2010/04/18/magazine/18marriage-t.html?_r=1&src=me&ref=general (4/30/2012).

4.   Daniel J. Siegel, "Toward an Interpersonal Neurobiology of the De-
     veloping Mind: Attachment Relationships, 'Mindsight,' and Neural
     Integration," *Infant Mental Health Journal* 22, nos. 1–2 (2001): 67–
     94; © Michigan Association for Infant Mental Health, p. 86.

5.   Linda J. Waite and Maggie Gallagher, *The Case for Marriage* (New
     York: Broadway Books, 2000), pp. 124–140; Wendy Manning and
     K. A. Lamb, "Adolescent Well-Being in Cohabitating, Married, and
     Single-Parent Families," *Journal of Marriage and the Family* 55 (4)
     2003, pp. 876–893.

6.   California Healthy Marriages Coalition, "Healthy Marriages,
     Healthy Children: Research on the Alignment of Marital Out-
     comes, Children's Psycho-Social Development, and Marriage Edu-
     cation," 2009; http://camarriage.com/content/resources/3a77fa16
     -7f58-493c-8cad-d1f373e50b7c.pdf 16–17; Linda J. Waite and Mag-
     gie Gallagher, *The Case for Marriage*, p. 124.

7.   Liz Weston, "Get Real: Marriage Is a Business," *MSN Money*, April 1,
     2011; http://money.msn.com/family-money/get-real-marriage-is-a
     -business-weston.aspx (4/30/2012).

8.   Joseph Lupton and James P. Smith, "Marriage, Assets, and Savings,"
     Labor and Population Program, Working Paper Series 99–12 (No-
     vember 1999), pp. 16–17.

9.   Waite and Gallagher, *The Case for Marriage*, pp. 78–83.

10. Parker-Pope, "Is Marriage Good for Your Health?"

Afterword

1.   Leah Hoffman, "To Have and to Hold Onto," *Forbes*, October
     7, 2006; http://www.forbes.com/2006/11/07/divorce-costs-legal-biz
     -cxlh1107legaldivorce.html (9/17/12).

2.   Benjamin Scafidi, principal investigator, "The Taxpayer Costs of Di-
     vorce and Unwed Childbearing: First-Ever Estimates for the Nation

and for All Fifty States," Institute for American Values, 2008; available at www.americanvalues.org, p. 20.

3. North Carolina Family Policy Council, "Landmark Study Estimates Costs of Family Fragmentation," April 16, 2008; http://ncfamily .org/stories/080416s1.html.

About the Authors and Imago Relationship Therapy

A former Baptist minister and university professor, Harville has more than forty years of experience as a clinical pastoral counselor, therapist, educator, clinical trainer, and public speaker on marriage and relationship therapy. Helen began her career as a high-school teacher in an economically depressed part of Dallas, which inspired her interest in promoting greater equality and healing in the world. She has cofounded several organizations and movements that promote women's and girl's equality. She met Harville, who was seeking to write about a new kind of marriage—an equal partnership marriage. They dated, and in time Helen proposed. Harville heartily accepted. And their marriage became the incubator for Imago Relationship Therapy.

Harville is the author of the *New York Times, USA Today,* and *Publishers Weekly* bestselling books *Getting the Love You Want: A Guide for Couples* and *Keeping the Love You Find: A Guide for Singles.* He and Helen have also co-authored seven books, including the bestselling *Giving the Love That Heals: A Guide for Parents.* In all, their books have been published in more than thirty-two languages, with more than three million copies in print worldwide.

They live in New York and have six children and five grand-children. And they are genuinely and truly happily married!

Imago Relationship Theory percolated in the minds and hearts of Harville and Helen for many years, and was officially co-created by them in the early 1980s. Harville's first appearance on *The Oprah Winfrey Show* in 1988 made her top twenty list of most influential moments. Oprah said that Imago Theory changed how she viewed her relationship, and she hinted that Imago Theory was ushering in a new kind of marriage.

The basic concept of Imago is that our primary relationship with our partner can—with the right tools—be a safe and sacred space. If we do the work of creating this kind of space, we not only build the relationship of our dreams but grow as individuals into a fuller, healthier, more fulfilled version of ourselves.

To help couples achieve fulfillment, Helen and Harville co-founded Imago Relationships International, a nonprofit organization whose mission is to create a new model of marriage and to transform the world—one relationship at a time. Presently there are more than 60,000 couples being helped annually by over 2,200 Imago Therapists practicing in 33 countries. There are also roughly 100 Imago educators, a new group of non-therapists passionate about spreading Imago throughout the world as well. And this number is growing daily.

Harville and Helen also bring the concepts of Imago to couples in workshops that they—and other Imago therapists—deliver worldwide.

You CAN create the marriage of your dreams!
We're here to help. . .

"We did it!"

You are not alone! You might have a nagging feeling that your relationship could be better. Maybe you're in a job transition or you're about to experience an empty nest—and you're wondering how to not only stay connected, but deepen your connection during this transition. Or it could be that you're in full-blown conflict. Whatever your relationship story is, it can have a happy ending.

And, if you'd like to take your journey a step further, there are ways to do that too!

- **Jumpstart your journey** with a weekend workshop!
- Access our digital library for **free downloads**.
- **Connect with others** who are using the ideas and exercises in this book in our **online community**.
- Check out **Harville & Helen's upcoming events**.
- **Find a therapist near you** and connect with one of the 2,200 Certified Imago Therapists around the world.
- Become a certified Imago Therapist and join an international community.

VISIT US AT
www.MakingMarriageSimple.com